H
Foucault's

How to Read Theory

Series Editors:
Stephen Shapiro, Department of English and
Comparative Literary Studies, University of Warwick
Ed White, Department of English, University of Florida

How to Read Theory is a new series of clear, introductory guides to critical theory and cultural studies classics designed to encourage readers to think independently. Each title focuses on a single, key text and concisely explains its arguments and significance, showing the contemporary relevance of theory and presenting difficult theoretical concepts in clear, jargon-free prose. Presented in a compact, user-friendly format, the How to Read Theory series is designed to appeal to students and to interested readers who are coming to these key texts for the first time.

Also available:

How to Read Marx's Capital
Stephen Shapiro

How to Read
Foucault's *Discipline and Punish*

Anne Schwan and Stephen Shapiro

PlutoPress
www.plutobooks.com

First published 2011 by Pluto Press
345 Archway Road, London N6 5AA

www.plutobooks.com

Distributed in the United States of America exclusively by
Palgrave Macmillan, a division of St. Martin's Press LLC,
175 Fifth Avenue, New York, NY 10010

British Library Cataloguing in Publication Data
A catalogue record for this book is available from the British Library

ISBN   978 0 7453 2981 9   Hardback
ISBN   978 0 7453 2980 2   Paperback

Library of Congress Cataloging in Publication Data applied for

This book is printed on paper suitable for recycling and made
from fully managed and sustained forest sources. Logging, pulping
and manufacturing processes are expected to conform to the
environmental standards of the country of origin.

10 9 8 7 6 5 4 3 2 1

Designed and produced for Pluto Press by Chase Publishing Services Ltd
Typeset from disk by Stanford DTP Services, Northampton, England
Simultaneously printed digitally by CPI Antony Rowe, Chippenham, UK
and Edwards Bros in the United States of America

Contents

Rationale

Another book on Foucault? Michel Foucault (1926–1984) is one of the most internationally influential French scholars of the post-World War II period. Known primarily for his work on the mutually enabling relationship between knowledge and power and their use for social control, Foucault has been so influential in the English-speaking humanities and social sciences that it is barely possible to consider yourself a serious student in these fields without a working understanding of his writing, concepts and terminology. Whether contemporary writers strongly agree or disagree with Foucault, or fall somewhere in between, nearly all respond to his widespread influence, even if many are, at times, themselves unaware of their dependence on it. Consequently, the number of books and articles that try to explain, use or extend Foucault is very long indeed. Why then, is there any need, at this late date, for a reader's guide to Foucault and one of his most-cited works, *Discipline and Punish: Birth of the Prison* (1975, English translation 1977)?

The *How to Read Theory* series has as its overall motive to fill a gap for new readers of theoretical classics who have been disserved over recent years. As 'theory' has become more commonly used in the humanities and social sciences, students have been increasingly taught these writings through selected key passages of larger works, usually in specially designed anthologies. This strategy, however, denies those new to theory the chance to *read* critical arguments in their full context. Anthology readers lose the chance to see the process by which an argument is built up or how they might even respond to somewhat prefabricated snippets. If those hostile to the presence of theory often complain that many writers use certain theoretical words and phrases as if they were magic incantations that could simply be sprinkled, with mesmeric spirit, over an essay as if they were self-evident truths, the anthology approach is partially to blame, no matter how well-intentioned its editors.

How to Read Theory, on the other hand, believes that unfamiliar readers are best educated when they are helped to understand the whole trajectory of an important work by exploring its overall careful construction. Without this complete horizon, readers risk isolating bits of an argument and then misunderstanding what a much-studied writer is trying to say.

Nowhere is this error of incompleteness more common than with Foucault in general and in particular, *Discipline and Punish*, one of his most significant works. Precisely because *Discipline and Punish* has been so cited, a great deal of writing on it is unhelpful, since English-speaking readers, who have frequently relied on secondary explanations and anthologies, do not realize the limits and errors these create. We feel that readers who want to benefit fully from Foucault's insights need to go back and read *Discipline and Punish* as a whole, paying attention to its actual claims and structure of argument, rather than the imaginary ones claimed for it. In particular, existing summaries of *Discipline and Punish* have been especially marred by three key absences, which we hope here to repair.

The first of these gaps is that abbreviated versions of *Discipline and Punish* lose sight that *Discipline and Punish* is above all a work of history emerging out of a particular French intellectual context. The book examines the strategy and tactics in punishment's changing forms from the late seventeenth and early eighteenth century to the mid nineteenth (and beyond). Yet when Foucault published his work, there was still a large difference, if not mutual hostility, between the kinds of historical writing that were dominant in English-speaking lands and the ones by French scholars, who were challenging the themes and methods that Anglophone historians favoured. One feature of this split was the French scholars' move away from defining history by great (usually) men and towards the study of a social history of anonymous or non-heroic figures, those often overlooked from academic perspectives, namely the working class and the poor, women, rural labourers, 'deviants' and criminals (these being overlapping categories). Another feature of the French historians was a declining commitment to relying on specific monumental dates, like those of battles, and towards longer periods of time, by taking several decades, or even centuries, as a single unit or by choosing dates that are not immediately dependent on the actions of a small group of elite historical figures. Even when Anglophone left and labour historians did begin to produce histories of the disempowered, they still tended to highlight 'events' rather than longer time-spans.

Because Foucault's work falls generally within these French interests, his work was largely introduced into the United States and the United Kingdom by literature, rather than history, professors. While the former were more accepting of Foucault's concerns, they were, conversely, often less interested in the historical phases that Foucault described and what helped create these changes. They focused instead mainly on the most recent historical phase that might be useful as a way to interpret modern literary and cultural affairs. By ignoring the several shifts between periods of time that Foucault describes, literary and cultural studies scholars lost sense of his claim about how modes of punishment carry meaning only in context of their own moment's dominant features and tensions. Yet if we are not attentive to Foucault's descriptions of ways in which Western societies developed into their modern forms, then we lose sight of both the present as a moment in an ongoing process and Foucault's, admittedly often implicit, suggestions for how we might move beyond or escape this present. Furthermore, if readers only examine parts of *Discipline and Punish*, then they can easily experience Foucault's vision as grim and lacking in change. Nothing could be further from the book's message. Yet to uncover Foucault's dedication to the possibility of a post-disciplinary society, we must pay close attention to his tale of passages through different historical moments to see what Foucault highlights as integral to the making of social change.

In one sense, *Discipline and Punish* appears easy to read. Large parts of the book are written with great style and draw on graphic, immediately understandable examples. Furthermore, the book is organized into parts and sections that make it easy to outline, especially as Foucault often numbers the points he wants to make. Additionally, Foucault is usually very careful to use his terminology in a precise and consistent fashion to differentiate the concepts he wants to illustrate. In another sense, though, Foucault can be an elusive writer to comprehend. This difficulty arises because Foucault was very much a member of the post-war French intellectual milieu. In the hothouse of universities located in and around Paris, academics were usually quite familiar with each other's positions within a set of well-known theoretical debates. Because of this (at times suffocating) proximity, they were able to develop a writing style that signalled their own position with a few casual words.

For readers who are less familiar with this French academic environment and its questions, it is very easy to overlook what might seem to be a marginal comment, but is, in fact, the key to decoding a particular passage. For instance, while many would expect that any social history of France throughout the eighteenth and nineteenth centuries would draw heavily on the Revolution's effects in the 1790s, Foucault, for reasons partly explained below, rarely draws his readers' attention to it. This is partly because Foucault assumes that his reader is French and therefore very familiar with their own political history, especially the period surrounding the French Revolution and modern nationhood. Many contemporary English-language readers of Foucault are simply not as well versed with these events and their representative figures. When this absence is combined with Foucault's light touch allusions to other academic arguments, large and important aspects of *Discipline and Punish* seem vague, marginal and skippable. Conversely, one reason why the segment on English political scientist Jeremy Bentham's plan for a new model prison, the Panopticon, is so commonly anthologized may be that it is a section that unusually deals with English-language material from an author whose name is already recognizable and has accompanying illustrations that make Foucault's point very clear. Yet the Panopticon section might arguably have been removed entirely from the book, since this segment mainly repeats points that Foucault has already made previously in the text. However, because English readers do not follow the historical tale that Foucault constructs or know the story of the French Revolution, they tend to lean on the Panopticon section in ways that create idiosyncratic explanations based on a limited perspective of *Discipline and Punish*.

Foucault might not have spoken more explicitly about the Revolution for reasons involving the second absence in most Anglophone discussions: Foucault's relationship with Marx. For most of the twentieth century, marxism was one of the main intellectual currents for European writers. Whether authors considered themselves on the right or the left, nearly every one wrote with an awareness of Marx's writing on political economy. Additionally, the Communist Party was a mass political party in post-war France and Italy. For English-speakers, the ubiquity of academic conversation about Marx and the wide-spread influence of the Stalinist-oriented French Communist Party (PCF) for much of the twentieth century's intellectual affairs is hard to grasp, given the historically marginal place the Communist Party has had in the UK and the US, as well as the fashion in recent decades to be anti-marxist. Writing after the 1960s, when the French Communist Party was condemned for being a retarding force on worker and student resistance, Foucault (himself briefly a Communist party member in the 1950s) often strives to distance himself from the PCF's official party line and associated theoretical concepts. By rarely mentioning the French Revolution, which had become a litmus test regarding one's allegiance to PCF dictates, Foucault indicates his desire to put distance between the party and himself. Since the French Revolution was read by the official left as allegorically foreshadowing the Russian one in 1918, and, in turn, the Cold War conflict between Western state-officiated capitalism and Eastern state-officiated sovietism, any mention of the 1790s was fraught. So if Foucault does not devote much time to the Revolution, it is because he wishes to avoid being seen as embroiled within the skirmishes surrounding party affiliation. And, as we will see, Foucault believes that state party politics obscure the ways in which modern power relations and class stratification operate.

Yet to move away from the official communist party is not the same as rejecting Marx's writings and insights. Marx is one of the most favourably cited authorities in *Discipline and Punish*, and Foucault implicitly and explicitly draws on Marx's arguments in *Capital* to help explain the logic for historical change. Foucault always introduces Marx as supporting evidence and never as a figure to be disproved. As Foucault makes clear (221), capitalism could not exist without the form of control that Foucault calls 'discipline' and discipline could not succeed without the rise of capitalism. In many ways, one of *Discipline and Punish*'s main projects in its treatment of class-struggle, power and knowledge is to provide a way for new students of Marx to escape the PCF's increasingly unfruitful use of the terms 'ideology' and 'false consciousness' as explanations for why the working class submits to middle-class authority.

Still, because so many Anglophone critics who used theory from the 1970s onward either explicitly positioned themselves as anti-marxist or were, more commonly, simply unfamiliar with Marx's work, they promoted readings of Foucault that denied or downplayed Foucault's agreements with Marx. Similarly, many unashamed marxists mistook the assertions of Foucault's acolytes for Foucault's own arguments, and they, too, (wrongly) insist that Foucault is unsympathetic to materialist claims. We feel that any basic reading of *Discipline and Punish* makes it impossible to claim any of the above. Therefore, our second justification for this book is the need to scrape away the crust of prejudice that has accumulated around *Discipline and Punish* in order to see afresh what it is actually arguing. As Foucault repeatedly asks us to do, we need to restore our reading of *Discipline and Punish* alongside Marx's critique of capitalism.

At its heart, *Discipline and Punish* is a stunning dismantling of the cherished bourgeois ideal of the individual and the political, economic and cultural valences of that concept. Liberal politics enshrines the rights of the individual at the heart of most of its constitutional and legal theories and actively seeks to make collective groupings, like class or ethnicity, invisible and unremarkable. The liberal notion of intrinsic basic freedoms depends on the assumption that it is the individual's speech and beliefs that must be protected against society. The individual also lies at the heart of liberal economic theory, which highlights the moment of the contract, the buying and selling between two consenting parties, as the most fair and equal way of conducting business exchanges. Culturally, the private individual is celebrated as the hallmark of Enlightenment rationality, humanist sensibility, the Romantic cult of artistic genius and the container of authentic, emotional and behavioural identities.

Along with a longstanding leftist and marxist tradition, Foucault uses *Discipline and Punish* to argue that the cultivation of the individual in these terms camouflages the middle class's desire to become the dominant group within a capitalist economy. The scene of the contract obscures actual power inequalities, Enlightenment reason is linked to coercive force and the humanist mythos of the authentic personality of the individual has been historically constructed as a device to control threatening collectives, namely those of the working and lower classes. Yet as Foucault casts suspicion on the humanist rhetoric of individual freedom, he challenges basic mainstream assumptions about using personal identity as a tool for liberation.

Here we find a third absence in many readings of Foucault. Because Foucault focuses on dominant social structures, it is easy to believe that he presents a totalizing vision, a picture of a closed box with no way out. This pessimistic reading can only come about from de-historicized and de-contextualized readings of Foucault's work. Foucault, however, repeatedly argues that each historical phase can and does decline, usually from its inability to control popular resistance from the lower and labouring classes. If discipline remains effective today, this is only because it has not fully been challenged, and it remains so effective as it works in ways almost unseen in our daily lives. Yet Foucault's ultimate motivation is to clarify how discipline operates so that it *can* be challenged. He is more forthright about this process, however, in his interviews, rather than in *Discipline and Punish* itself.

Nowhere does Foucault present a monolithic version of society or suggest that left political activism is pointless. Foucault wrote *Discipline and Punish* alongside his own membership in *GIP* (*Le Groupe d'Information sur les*

Prisons/Group for Information on Prisons), which sought to provide a public medium for French prisoners' complaints at a time when prisoners' riots for rights were making the news. Elsewhere in his writing, Foucault talks about the need for academic researchers to recover the voices of the historically disempowered to help better contemporary conditions. *Discipline and Punish* belongs to this vision. When Foucault says that he is writing 'the history of the present' (31), he invites his contemporary readers to *use* the lessons of his history, not simply learn them by heart.

These three elements of (revolutionary) history, marxism and activism are often muted in accounts of Foucault, yet without them, no intelligible or satisfying reading of *Discipline and Punish* can emerge. Our goal here is to be 'new' only by maintaining fidelity to Foucault's actual text.

Overview

In *Discipline and Punish*, Foucault presents a history of the changes in criminal codes and punishments to explore why Western society moved from a bodily punishment of torture to a 'gentle' punishment of prison sentences. He argues that we did not stop torturing people because we became more enlightened, humanitarian and respectful of individual rights. Instead, he claims that the codes of 'justice' always represent and materially enact social power. The difference between early modern society and a modern one is not that modern society is more civilized; it is just that punishment before the late eighteenth century had a logic that expressed the dominant interests of society wherein the King was meant to have absolute power. Punishment in modern society is enacted differently because modern society is bourgeois; it is controlled by the middle class, and the middle class has different social agendas than the monarchy.

Foucault focuses on a history of punishment, therefore, to illustrate the larger social transfer and transformation of power from the aristocracy to the middle classes. By learning the changes in the mode of punishment over time, we can see how since the late eighteenth/early nineteenth century, the bourgeoisie have maintained authority by creating modern forms of subjectivity through a dual process: making an individual a non-threatening, subordinated political 'subject' while simultaneously installing a new kind of personhood or identity. This form of power mainly works by producing *knowledge*, a defining 'truth' about individuals' behaviour and personality, only in order to *discipline* them through *social definitions of normality*, *material institutions* (like schools, hospitals and prison reformatories) and the supervising judgment of *professionals* (doctors, teachers, judges, etc.). The story Foucault tells is the move from excessive public, physical punishments to private, invisible discipline of our psychological sense of selfhood, as a middle-class tactic to control forms of popular (mass) socialization and alternative political and economic outlooks.

By challenging the notion that the 'self' is a space of human freedom and guarantee of rights, Foucault seeks to dismantle cherished notions about political and economic liberalism, which highlight individual choice and liberty; the Enlightenment, as a movement that believes that knowledge can be objective and detached from power relations, if not actively in opposition to social inequality; and all forms of psychological claims that believe we have an authentic interior personality that is an aesthetic sanctuary from the public realm of politics and the marketplace.

Discipline and Punish, then, uses penal history to incriminate a host of Enlightenment and Romantic-era claims about society and the self. Rather than seeing the personal as a tool of liberation, Foucault sees it as a trap that has been set in advance for us by middle-class interests. As such, Foucault seems to be offering a critique from within the left about the ways in which the cultural politics of the 1960s onward have been organized along the lines of (ethnic, racial, sexual, gender, environmental, etc.) identity politics and claims for self-expression. In critiquing the self's desires as socially conditioned and contaminated by social divisions and economic inequality, Foucault also offers a line of critical enquiry on all forms of humanities and social science scholarship that often take these new kinds of identities as their focus. This approach became especially evident in literary studies, where the idea of individual genius and the heroic reader's private pleasure had been a dominant theme for some time, a move that Foucault specifically mentions in *Discipline and Punish*. What if novels, for instance, are themselves mediums for transmitting unfair power relations as they help audiences to fashion their imagination about the self?

In *Discipline and Punish*, Foucault reveals knowledge, power and subjectivity as a scheme that often operates below our radar, since its procedures usually seem trivial and not worth protesting. In *How to Read Foucault's Discipline and Punish*, we seek to enable the reader's efforts in their first encounter with this challenging and exciting book. To help orient you, we follow *Discipline and Punish*'s chapter and section structure and often quote Foucault's own words so that they will seem less strange or incomprehensible when you next read them. We try to be comprehensive in our account, but no guide can ever be complete. Foucault is too complex a thinker and the riches of *Discipline and Punish* can only be found through multiple readings. Ideally this book will help provide the platform for these future encounters, assisting you with the first steps by pointing out the book's general architecture and significance of its passages. With this awareness, you should be more comfortable and confident in reading (and using) *Discipline and Punish* and Foucault's other writings as well. In short, this guide should be a starting point, not a conclusion.

Note on Text

Foucault originally published *Surveiller et Punir: Naissance de la Prison* in 1975 with Éditions Gallimard. The first and only English translation, by Alan Sheridan, appeared in 1977 with Allen Lane. While this translation has since appeared under different imprints (UK readers will usually find it as a Penguin, while it is Vintage for US ones), the plates and pagination remain the same for all. Any Anglophone reader can thus easily locate the pages indicated in our parenthetical references.

There are two main formal differences between the French original and the English translation. More illustrative plates are included in the former, mostly of different images of prisons. Also, Sheridan turned some of the non-descriptive footnote citations into embedded parenthetical references. We believe that Sheridan's change makes for a more fluid reading experience. In his translator's note, Sheridan comments on the work's title, which literally would be *To Survey and Punish*. After Foucault, we might find the word 'surveillance' easier to understand and more rich in implications, but in the 1970s, Sheridan found it 'too restricted and technical'. He claims that Foucault himself suggested the English title as the best compromise. Lastly, when Foucault talks about abstract individuals, he only uses the masculine pronoun. Contemporary readers may see this as either simply a convention of Foucault's time or a dogged inability to recognize the implication of gender. In any case, we will below typically use 'he or she' and so on.

In memory of Sally Ledger (1961–2009), Melvin Shapiro (1927–2009) and Mitzi Shapiro (1933–2010).

Part One: Torture

The first section of the first part of *Discipline and Punish* acts as an overview of the book's argument. Here Foucault outlines his main themes and makes some, perhaps overly, brief comments on the assumptions driving his method of interpreting historical evidence. On first reading, this is one of the book's most dense and at times elusive sections. Consequently, it is helpful to re-read it after having read through to the end of *Discipline and Punish* so that you can begin to notice the moves that Foucault makes and positions he takes very early on in the book.

As we will see, Foucault divides his history of prisons into three historical phases, some of which overlap with one another, causing him sometimes to repeat points in different sections. In general, though, each of the book's first three parts is devoted to a particular period, with Part Four as his critical overview and summary. In the second section of Part One, Foucault details the first of these three phases, what we might call the Age of Terror.

1. The body of the condemned

Discipline and Punish begins by contrasting two visions of criminal punishment: the 1757 public execution of Robert-François Damiens (1715–1757) for an attempted assassination of the French King Louis XV and the 1838 daily schedule for prisoners' activities proposed by the journalist, and later centre-right French minister for the Interior, Léon Faucher (1803–1854).

Foucault starts with contemporaneous newspaper accounts of Damiens' gruesome death. After Damiens was publicly branded with red-hot irons, flesh torn away and body drawn and quartered, as horses ripped the limbs away from his torso, he was finally burnt alive. Against this horrifying, excessive carnival of an individual's suffering, Faucher's calmly regulated plan for the prisoners' day appears to handle criminals in a more dignified and reasonable way, one that carefully avoids chaotic scenes and screams of human pain.

Foucault chooses to contrast the 'public execution and a time-table' (7) as the two overarching markers in his study about changes within the history of punishment. He acknowledges that these two moments are not exactly comparable as items of representative evidence, since they deal with different kinds of crime, the attempted murder of a king, on one hand, and most likely small thefts or disorderly conduct, on the other. Yet the examples of a king's would-be murderer and plans for anonymous men imprisoned for minor crimes neatly captures three larger themes that Foucault highlights throughout *Discipline and Punish*, involving the links among subjectivity, knowledge and power. Foucault argues that during the eighty years separating these scenes 'the entire economy of punishment was redistributed' (7). In the interval between these two events, a wave of prison reform swept across the West as these societies lost their tolerance for circus-like open-air spectacles where the 'tortured, dismembered, amputated body, symbolically branded on face or shoulder' was 'exposed alive or dead to public view' (8). Although Foucault's illustrations are almost entirely French ones, he argues that they are representative of a 'Western' general trend throughout Europe (including Russia) and North America.

While most histories of penal justice celebrate the removal of apparently senseless, grotesque punishment of criminals in favour of rational codes of law, involving juries and time-delimited imprisonment, as an humanitarian advance, Foucault suggests that before we rush to congratulate ourselves on this removal of public torture, we need to pay attention to what social interests motivated the disappearance of the body as 'the major target of penal repression' within a 'gloomy festival of punishment' (8) at the end of the eighteenth and early nineteenth centuries. There are two significant features to this historical shift.

Firstly, there 'was the disappearance of punishment as spectacle' (8), such as when prisoners were either brought on top of a platform for public retribution or forced to labour in easily visible chain-gangs cleaning the streets or repairing roads. Enlightenment-era reformers were increasingly worried that public executions might encourage a shocked public to commit violence against authorities, given the open cruelty of the older forms of punishment that made justice seem itself criminal-minded and uncivilized. Consequently, reformers used a 'humanitarian' language to argue for a less aggressive and risky way of treating criminals.

In this light, the second main change in punishment is the removal of pain. The modern 'punishment-body relation' (11) seeks to cause less bodily hurt and looks more to deprive someone of 'a liberty that is regarded as a right and as property' involving limits to free movement and use of the individual's time. The 'outside' of the criminal's body is handled less and less as it becomes manipulated more intangibly and peacefully through confinement. Even when people are executed in the modern-day West, 'the disappearance of the spectacle and the elimination of pain' (11) remains a concern, as death sentences are usually carried out before small, invitation-only audiences and the prisoner is often either sedated before being killed or every effort is made for the death to be swift and 'gentle'.

The change in punishment's form from spectacular, public punishment in the mid eighteenth century to more discreet forms of imprisonment in the early and mid nineteenth century has several social and tactical consequences, according to Foucault. With imprisonment, punishment becomes more 'private', isolated and hidden from the public's gaze. While the performance of deliberative justice, the judging of guilt, becomes more visible, as trials are usually open to all and performed in the public record (whereas before they were secret), the execution of that trial's punishment becomes more invisible, especially since few of us step inside a penitentiary, which, in any case, cannot easily be visited without some degree of permission by state officials or guards.

The effect of this privatization of punishment is that the act of punishment becomes more abstract to us. The move from the 'visible intensity' of publicly displayed acts, like Damiens' death, open to 'more or less everyday perception' (9), to punishment's enactment in spaces hidden from our view, means that we must increasingly imagine, rather than watch, punishment happening and so begin to internalize its activity within our mental consciousness. Once punishment is no longer a commonly witnessed experience of a momentary, physical event in a public space, but stands as a time-based process that we must intuitively imagine, it begins to implant its effect within all of our imaginations. Rather than simply being limited to the poor figure being torn to pieces or broken on the public scaffold, the location of punishment is transferred so that it now unfolds within our collective minds, rather than on a single anatomy.

The less visible and 'corporal' punishment becomes, the easier it is for justice authorities to shift the responsibility for punishment away from themselves. When someone like Damiens is executed, justice 'takes public responsibility for the violence that is bound up with its practice' (9), as a central executioner does the actual damage of justice on the criminal while everyone watches. The 'horror' of the scaffold binds executioner and criminal together in a repetition of the punished crime, this time reversed, since the violence is done to, rather than by, the criminal. If the crowd feels that the punishment is unfair, then they easily know who to blame and attack. Within the modern reform of punishment, authorities become more reluctant to be seen as the source that duplicates criminal violence; they become 'ashamed' to kill or cause harm (9). Authorities now say that they have no 'desire to punish' and destroy the criminal; instead they claim that punishment is used to 'correct, reclaim, "cure"' and improve the accused (10). They claim to seek the prisoner's reform, not enact revenge.

As punishment becomes 'gentle', the responsibility for recuperating or curing the criminal becomes dispersed among several bureaucratic agencies. Judges are no longer held as the sole author of the sentence. Instead, they are protectively surrounded by 'minor civil servants of moral orthopaedics' (10), like psychologists and social workers, who cluster around the judge's bench to advise on the severity of punishment. This swarming reduces the burden or culpability any single individual must carry for punishing someone:

> As a result of this new restraint, a whole army of technicians took over from the executioner, the immediate anatomist of pain: warders, doctors, chaplains, psychiatrists, psychologists, educationalists; by their very presence near the prisoner, they sing the praises that the law needs: they reassure it that the body and pain are not the ultimate objects of its punitive action. (11)

The effect of this decentralization of justice is the creation of a bureaucratic network where the figures that have power over individuals can sanitize or deny their responsibility for enacting punishment. In this way, the guillotine acts as a marker of transition, since it was initially seen as a good replacement for hanging because the machine removed the need for any specific human to be seen touching, and thus taking blame, for the criminal's death (13). Both the impact on the convict's body and on the executioner's responsibility are here 'reduced to a split second' (13). The interiorization and making-innocent of punishment through decentralization, and changes in technologies of punishment, is both a hallmark of the move to modernity away from pre- or early modern society and the first of Foucault's main themes in the book.

The second main theme of *Discipline and Punish* involves the relationship between Enlightenment humanism, social sciences and political control: the link between knowledge and power. Foucault chooses to begin

Discipline and Punish with these two scenes, one in 1757 and the other in the mid nineteenth century, because they typify the historical changes that he considers occurring roughly between the 'great transformation of the years 1760–1840' (15). Although Foucault does not explicitly give a citation for this phrase and periodization, he is silently referring to *The Great Transformation* (1944), a study of the capitalist market's rise by Hungarian economic historian and sociologist Karl Polanyi (1886–1964). In this work, Polanyi criticizes the beliefs of classical political economy, represented by the writing of Adam Smith, who believes that a 'free' market economy can best develop alone and without any state regulation or governmental oversight. Polanyi, instead, argues that a capitalist market economy could only have arisen through protection and nurturing by the modern nation-state. Throughout his career, Polanyi also rejected the notion that the economy is determined by rational individuals' response to supply and demand; instead, he argued that economics is always shaped by social considerations and organized by collective institutional forces.

By using Polanyi's phrase, which Foucault assumes is well known and easily recognized by his readers, he silently indicates that the examples of Damiens and Faucher are not as randomly chosen as they might initially seem. Firstly, these events represent the markers between different historical periods of social organization, for Damiens belongs to the period of the absolutist state when the hereditary monarch monopolized power. The journalist and minister under Louis-Napoleon, Faucher, belongs to the high point of France's development as a leading capitalist nation ruled by a constitutional monarch alongside a bureaucratic civil service and political party parliament.

As Foucault begins with these two anecdotes, one from the *Ancien Régime* kingdom in the years just before the French Revolution and the other from within a nation-state dominated by middle-class interests in the years after the Revolution and Napoleon, Foucault implies that he will be using his history of punishment as a way of commenting on the transformation of French (and Western) society from the post-feudal, early modern period towards modern formations. Foucault might not mention Polanyi by name, but by so clearly invoking the title of Polanyi's famous book, Foucault suggests that he, too, is interested in examining the institutional support and complement to capitalist economics in ways that reject both a political science of the free market and a kind of (Stalinist/PCF) marxist outlook that is too focused on a narrow interpretation of economics.

The choice of a study about the removal of corporal punishment and rise of the penitentiary gives a preliminary indication of Foucault's Polanyi-like intervention. The removal of public executions and scenes of pain stands as one of the most celebrated examples of the rise of enlightened democracy that replaced aristocratic and monarchical despotism and rule through arbitrary force by reason through legal codes and contracts. Foucault suggests that the shift from corporal to gentle punishment within the context of the rise of middle-class society is accompanied by the rise of the social sciences and humanities, forms of knowledge that are often considered to be separate or free from the market place. If Polanyi argues that the marketplace cannot be considered in isolation from governmental politics, Foucault similarly analyses the necessary relationship between new 'humane' practices and the fashioning of new modes of political subjectivity.

Here we should also note Foucault's careful acknowledgement of potential replies to his larger historical argument about the disappearance of 'the great spectacle of physical punishment' where 'the tortured body was avoided; the theatrical representation of pain was excluded from punishment' (14). He does not suggest that at some imaginary date the West instantly woke up and for evermore stopped hanging people or inflicting physical pain. He acknowledges that the transformation between different historical periods is both an uneven process and one that has overlapping practices. For instance, some of the older rituals of public punishment were grafted onto newer practices. And older forms of criminal punishment occasionally returned in different places and times and were context-dependent. England 'did not wish to diminish the rigour of her penal laws during the great social disturbances of the years 1780–1820' and the number of executions rose just as other places were making punishment more lenient (14). Similarly, 'at the time of the counter-revolutions in Europe and the great social fear of the years 1820–1848', prison reform began to retreat. These dates suggest that at times of popular unrest, authorities did not hesitate to return to more coercive and physically abrasive forms of punishment. Just as Foucault admits that the pathway towards modernity is often irregular, he also acknowledges that even today there is a physical aspect of pain, a 'trace of "torture"' within modern imprisonment, since it would be hard to imagine a purely 'non-corporal punishment' (16). Violence is never entirely absent even in the 'humanitarian' environment.

Yet Foucault insists that despite such residues or occasional returns to older forms and mechanisms, the overall trajectory was towards a less spectacular and pain-driven punishment. If there are periods like the English one mentioned above, Foucault will implicitly explain them with regards to the rise of political resistance and rebellion by the labouring classes against the emerging forms of the modern nation-state and market economy. This connection between capitalist class warfare and social transformation is Foucault's third, and concluding, main theme in *Discipline and Punish*.

After having outlined the main themes of the study, Foucault then suggests that his purpose in *Discipline and Punish* is to relate 'a correlative history of the modern soul and of a new power to judge' (23). In other words, rather than assuming that we have always had a sense of our interior self, our soul, he will argue that this sense of personal identity has been socially conditioned and historically constructed. Furthermore, this feeling of individual personhood will be shown to arise through new forms of evaluating behaviour. Hence, while we might consider our self as purely 'natural', 'authentic' and untouched by society, Foucault claims that it is a product of modern examination. Foucault uses this book to investigate the source of these influences.

The important shift in the last two hundred years, then, is not the superficial reduction of penal severity and increased desire to respect the human rights of prisoners, but that the punishment's *objective*, its object or target of operation, has changed. Punishment no longer wants to handle the outside body, but instead wants to get *inside* the prisoner to consider and impact the prisoner's heart, mind, will and inclinations: in short, the criminal's *soul*. In this turn, we have shifted from a tragic 'spectacle of punishment, the body and the blood' (16), ending with the criminal's mortal destruction, to a desire to improve a 'bodiless reality' through a new 'apparatus of punitive justice' (17). In this transition, certain crimes began to decrease in seriousness, like the ones of blasphemy or smuggling, but these changes have not removed the barrier between 'the permitted and the forbidden'. What the law now criminalizes has simply shifted to foreground the source and different kinds of crime, namely a new realm of more psychological violations, the 'extenuating circumstances of the 'passions, instincts, anomalies, infirmities, maladjustments, effects of environment or heredity...aggressivity...perversions... drives and desires' (17). Instead of asking the accused 'what did you do', the law now asks, 'what are you?'

The effect of this change is that punishment increasingly wants to receive and create *knowledge* about the prisoner. The change in the target of punishment results, therefore, in a new object of information gathering. As mentioned, the relation between knowledge and power is one of *Discipline and Punish*'s main themes as Foucault considers the larger historical transformation from a later phase of the early modern period (up to roughly the mid eighteenth century) to a more modern one (emerging in the late eighteenth through mid nineteenth century). In the earlier period, the *act* of crime was the object of punishment. Previously, justices did not question why someone may have committed a crime; they were mainly concerned with determining the existence of a guilty deed and how to punish that act. In the modern period, a person's 'will', his or her intentions, motivations and influences for committing crime are the main concerns. This turn from punishment as vengeful compensation for a crime to a means of preventing or neutralizing 'criminal tendencies', the move of focus from act to personality and desire involves a fusion between medicine and jurisprudence that will create a new *domain*, or field, of 'scientific knowledge', like criminal anthropology, the sociology of deviancy and psychology of perversion.

In this process, judges now do 'something other than pass judgment' (19). In the earlier system, justices sought to establish if an offence occurred, who committed the crime, and what was the appropriate punishment for that crime. In the modern one, justices examine the 'causal process' or background to the crime (was the criminal mad? from a deprived background? etc.) as a means of rehabilitating the criminal, of changing their future development. The move from determining the act to evaluating the criminal's mentality means that a new set of questions and operations enters into legal discussions. The modern criminal system now needs to have a means of determining the absence of criminal predispositions. The modern system has to create a 'set of assessing, diagnostic, prognostic, normative judgments' that can help determine what are the normal ways of life against which crime can be differentiated. The justice system additionally seeks to produce ostensibly neutral, objective (quantitative) standards that gauge the reform of a person's negative and dangerous qualities.

From this search for normative judgments that can diagnose and predict the criminal's behaviour in ways according to standard models or norms, a new, distinctively modern 'scientifico-juridical complex' (19) emerges, by which Foucault means the ways in which new forms of scientific knowledge about criminal behaviour and legal judgments converge. One example of this turn involves the relationship of madness to criminality. Previously the question of a criminal's insanity was irrelevant when the main concern was simply to determine if a crime had been committed. A new criminology that organizes itself around the interior mentality of an accused must, however, take the question of a person's insanity seriously, since its presence will impact what kind of corrective punishment is meted out. Depending on whether insanity is seen as something that can be cured or not, there will need to be two different kinds of penal institutions: one for the 'criminally insane' and another for those whose personalities can be reformed in ways that allow for criminals to be paroled.

Foucault argues that the modern court does more than judge guilt; the judge gives an 'assessment of normality and a technical prescription for a possible normalization' (21), that is the court now assesses how best to rehabilitate the offender into standardized forms of social behaviour. In this new role of adjudicating motive and personality, the judge no longer sits imperiously alone on the bench as '[t]hroughout the penal procedure and the implementation of the sentence there swarms a whole series of subsidiary authorities' like 'psychiatric or psychological experts...educationalists, members of the prison service' (21). A 'whole machinery' (21) arises that decentralizes or fragments the originating authority of the sentence. This 'new penal system' (22) not only expands the range of what the judge considers, but it also increases the number of people involved in determining the sentence and what they can comment on about the accused when fixing the penal judgment. The displacement of authority from the judge, as the sole source of responsibility, to a host of 'extra-juridical elements and personnel' (22), who assist in giving advice to the judge, consequently means that a 'whole new system of truth and a mass of roles hitherto unknown' (23) has entered criminal justice. As these new figures bring in new ways of analysing the accused, they introduce new 'truths' or 'knowledges', mainly those involving the mind or psychology.

In his words, Foucault is writing a 'genealogy', not in the sense of showing the lineage of concepts, as would be the case for a traditional history of ideas approach, but to show how ideas developed (in the sense of genesis, of being created) through specific historical events and social influences. The target of his genealogy is the 'present scientifico-legal complex from which the power to punish derives its bases, justifications and rules' (23). By using the word 'present', Foucault here stresses once more his ultimate motivation to expose how contemporary social formations were historically constructed and he implies that they can therefore be changed. If punishment seems more lenient today and less brutal than it was in the early eighteenth century, this is only because modern society organizes social control through institutional judgments on our interior personality, rather than primarily inflicting pain on our flesh.

On first glance, Foucault's claim that our sense of selfhood is a policed realm is unsettling, since we typically like to consider that a public/private divide exists: outside there is society, which is false and full of constraints, but there is an inside, wherein lies our true self, the 'real me', which is the more authentic, vibrant and uncontaminated sphere. Foucault not only refuses this separation, but also argues that the very idea of this self is bound up with the 'new power to judge' that finds its most explicit formulation around criminality. In a larger sense, then, while a history of prisons might seem a somewhat dry or minor theme, one of not much interest beyond a small circle of specialist academics or civil servants, Foucault uses this theme as his tool to enquire about the larger notion of the modern self, the formation of the idea that we have an intrinsic personality that is at once original and capable of being improved, that there is an interior realm where we can 'find' ourselves. Foucault disagrees; he sees the invention of the self as a trap, a field fraught with power relations, especially as it is riven with a 'corpus of knowledge, techniques, "scientific" discourses' that 'is formed and becomes entangled with the practice of power to punish' (23), rather than personal liberation.

In this sense, Foucault is a 'posthumanist', one who critiques the definitions of individuality that lie at the core of the humanist justifications for society. To say this about Foucault does not mean that he lacks ethical considerations for people. He clearly does, but wants to encourage his readers to recognize how what seems to be a liberating concept – our self – is shot through with power relations that were fundamentally developed to prevent collective human liberation. He wants us to go beyond the concept of 'the human' in order to grasp at real social emancipation. Similarly, he is also 'post-Enlightenment' for much the same reasons. He sees Enlightenment claims to the disinterested discovery of knowledge as having a sinister side, where the pursuit of 'truth' is the companion to the desire for social control, often to the effect of excluding alternative perspectives.

But to cast suspicion on the effects of knowledge-production is not to believe that anything goes or that anything can be said. Consequently, Foucault ends this mini section with some reflections on the method of enquiry that he will use for his 'history of the modern soul on trial' (23) and how he considers his approach to be different and distinctive from prior ones. He wants to argue that classical sociologists, like Émile Durkheim (1858–1917), have replaced effect with cause. In the essay, 'Two Laws on Penal Evolution' (1899–1900), Durkheim argues something descriptively similar to Foucault. He proposes the presence of two 'laws' that combine the numerical and experiential, the quantitative and qualitative. Durkheim's first 'law' is that punishment is more violent and 'intense' in less developed societies, which tend to centralize power in absolutist and theocratic governments. The second law is that more developed societies increasingly use limitations on the freedom of time (imprisonment) as their chief punishment. Durkheim's overall explanation for this historical change from the premodern to modern forms of punishment is the rise of individualization.

According to Durkheim, early societies were more collective in nature, so that crime was an affront to the whole social structure. Consequently, restrictive punishments, like prison sentences, were not used very much. There was little concern that an individual would flee from justice, since any punishment would simply be transferred to that person's kinship or clan group, who bear responsibility for all their members' actions. With the rise of the modern individual, who is no longer tied to social collectives, group-based shock and awe works less effectively. Thus, a new institutional form of punishment must be made, one that strikes at what every 'individual' ostensibly fears the most – the deprivation of personal liberty of movement – and is less violent, since 'advanced' societies have a greater sense of sympathetic reaction, that is we shirk when we see someone else's body damaged. Since 'modern' individuals are more easily scared, criminal sentences do not need to expend as much energy on the violence of torture and bodily pain, as only a little bodily control will serve the purpose.

As we will see, Foucault has a very similar argument about the changing form of punishment as it correlates to different kinds of institutional power regimes, with the move from the absolutist state to a modern, civil (bourgeois) society. But crucially, he thinks that Durkheim has made a mistake and misrecognized the originating factor that alters social forms. Durkheim argues that the rise of individual identity forces changes in penal law. Foucault, by contrast, thinks that individuality is 'one of the effects of the new tactics of power, among which are to be included the new penal mechanisms' (23). Durkheim believes that the modern individual makes changes; Foucault will argue that our sense of individual agency or autonomy is a form *through which* modern power mechanisms operate. The individual or soul is bound within power, not a key to unlock it. Foucault can thus be said to be even more socially oriented than even the founders of sociology.

After having distinguished himself from traditional sociology, Foucault now lists 'four general rules' of method that will differentiate his study from other fields, like political science. These very brief paragraphs are very deep in their implications, so much so that Foucault's next major book (and the other contender for consideration as his most influential work), *The History of Sexuality: Volume I* (1976, English translation 1978) spends most of its pages unpacking the four paragraphs on pages 23–4. These methodological rules are:

How to Read Foucault's *Discipline and Punish*

1. Don't think of punishment as something that only represses or says 'no'.

Think of punishment as a complex social function that *produces* effects (like the idea of crime) through society, even if these productions initially seem beside the point or slightly irrelevant. Foucault often treats aspects or events that may seem to be marginal and insignificant, but he will use them as an avenue towards unravelling a larger, 'complex social function' (23). Foucault returns to unpack this concept about not reading punishment as repressing social aspects in the last paragraphs of Part Two on page 194 and Part Four, Section 2, 'Illegalities and Delinquency'.

2. View punishment as a political tactic, a way of enacting power.

Don't think of punishment as simply the neutral result of objective laws; justice is never an 'innocent' concept. Foucault insists that punishment is always bound up within political struggles and is a means of exercising power. He rejects the idea that punishment is simply the bland consequence of disinterested legislation. Foucault sees punishment as a mechanism for the operation of power.

3. The history of penal law and the history of the human and social sciences are interrelated.

Rather than seeing human and social sciences as a field that only analyses or places limits on penal law, Foucault argues that the development of the human and social sciences and how they make statements about what is true is tied up with the changes in penal law. This point is similar to the one above (the supposed neutrality of the judicial system) as Foucault erases the distinction between the humanities and social sciences and power. Foucault sees 'the technology of power [as] the very principle both of the humanization of the penal system and of the knowledge of man' (23). Knowledge and power are intertwined. Neither the social sciences nor the humanities are free from complicity with social control.

Foucault rejects the idea that scientific rationality and humanitarian enlightenment stand outside of power and can act as the detergent that cleanses society from power's contamination. Instead, he sees the human and social sciences as part and symptoms of the new development of modern power relations. In the modern period, the making of truth-claims, of 'knowledge', will be itself a means of enacting power, not an escape from it. When Foucault uses the phrase 'epistemologico-juridical formation' (23), he implies that the means of determining truth or knowledge (epistemology) and punishment belong to the same formation. The same 'technology of power' underlines both 'the humanization of the penal system' and 'the knowledge of man' (23).

This scepticism about truth has a history going back to the eighteenth century, but here might come most directly from Friedrich Nietzsche's *On the Genealogy of Morals* (1887) that treats the inter-relation of truth, selfhood and criminal punishment. Nietzsche (1844–1900) argues that our moral concepts of good and evil are simply coded allegories for strong and weak. The powerful describe themselves as morally pure and condemn those whom they dominate as ethically damaged in order to justify the victimization of the weak. Nietzsche also argues that these distinctions can only continue to be used if they are first registered on the outside of our bodies, through pain, and then on our interior imaginations, through fear. While Nietzsche argues this through a combination of ancient philology and speculative philosophy, Foucault will do so using examples that are more recent and better documented through historical evidence. In this light, he declares his fourth rule.

4. The body is a field of power; it is invested by power relations.

Foucault considers the body as 'invested by power relations', alongside the 'entry of the soul on the scene of penal justice' and the insertion of 'scientific' knowledge within the system (24). Rather than ignoring the body as no longer important when punishment historically moves away from trying to cause physical pain on the body's surface, Foucault insists that the body remains important in the modern age, but its role is different. In the modern period, there is a metamorphosis in methods of punishment, but the ensuing 'change' in the use of the body is that it will be invested within a 'specific mode of subjection' (24). 'Subjection' implies a new way to create political and social subjects (human beings under different kinds of governmental rule and legislative codes) who are also 'subjected', that is dominated by those interests with greater social authority. Typically, the word 'ideology' has been used to describe the consent of the ruled to their domination. Foucault dislikes this term, not only because it suggests a model of repressive control that he has rejected with the first rule, but also because it seems to ignore the key role of the body in social relations. Foucault insists that we can only explore the landscape of social power by investigating the construction of embodiment, the ways in which subjectivity is tied to the body as well as the mind.

Before Foucault continues, with an unnumbered section break, he indicates in one of his rare, and hence very important, descriptive footnotes that he considers *Discipline and Punish* as following in the wake of other writers and works who share similar concerns. He names philosopher Gilles Deleuze and psychoanalyst Félix Guattari (co-authors of *Anti-Oedipus* (1972), to which Foucault wrote a preface acclaiming it as an introduction to a 'nonfascist life'); sociologist Robert Castel's still untranslated *Le Psychoanalysme: L'Ordre Psychanalytique et le Pouvoir* [Psychoanalysis: The Psychoanalytic Order and Power] (1973), which critiques the psychiatric profession (Castel's later work is also close to Foucault as it investigates social exclusion and the construction of waged-labour as a status identity); and historian Pierre Nora, associated with the 'new history' movement in France and now best known for his writing on the construction of French national memory through the construction of public monuments and organized celebrations. Foucault's debt to Nora is also more direct, since the latter was the general editor of the *Bibliothèque des Histoires*, the series that *Discipline and Punish* was published within. The mission statement for this series, included within the original French edition, but deleted in the English translation, declares its dedication to this new kind of history that Foucault clearly identifies with:

Until very recently, history was dedicated to the narration of events that struck contemporaries as significant, or the memory of great men and the political destiny of nations, but now it has changed its methods, its organization and its objects.... All of mankind, with its body, its foodways, its languages, it representations, its technological and mental instruments which change more or less rapidly, all that was once ignored or neglected, now becomes the daily bread of historians.

All of these writers and works referenced by Foucault are more or less contemporaneous with *Discipline and Punish*, which indicates the preoccupation in early 1970s France with questions about social cultural outlooks that fuse a history of ideas with sociological concerns about authority and subordination.

If Foucault differentiates himself from classical sociology represented by Durkheim (and aligns himself with a newer variant), he uses the next section break to discuss more at length his study's relationship to other kinds of left-wing history and sociology. First up is *Punishment and Social Structure* (1939), a marxist analysis of punishment. The first part of this text was based on a shorter work by Georg Rusche (1900–1941?), originally written in German and published in 1933 by the Frankfurt Institute of Social Research. When several Frankfurt School members, like Theodor Adorno (1903–1969), emigrated to the United States to escape the Nazis, they gave Rusche's manuscript to Otto Kirchheimer (1905–1965) who translated and supplemented Rusche's work, apparently with little consultation with Rusche, who had remained in Germany.

Foucault begins by reciting aspects of Rusche and Kirchheimer's study that he agrees with: the claim that we need to abandon the notion that punishment is 'above all (if not exclusively) a means of reducing crime' (24) and a process that seeks to make the criminal feel sorry or obtain redress for social damage. Instead we must analyse the '"concrete systems of punishment"...as social phenomena' that have deeper roots than simply reflecting ethical positions or the structure of the judiciary (24). Rusche and Kirchheimer argue that we must not consider punishment as something that simply is negative and seeks to prevent, exclude, or eliminate crime: the definition and presence of crime exists to produce 'a whole series of positive and useful effects' (24).

For Rusche and Kirchheimer, the punishment of crime always provides support for the current dominant mode of production. As students of Marx, they believe that society is mainly defined by the ways in which labour processes are divided in ways that create inequality and social tensions. Rusche and Kirchheimer consequently insist on a schematic, almost one to one, equation of different historical and social phases of production and relative cost of labour with the nature of criminal punishment. In the economies of the classical period, like that of Rome, states desperately needed labourers to provide food through large farms. In the absence of imperial war that brought conquered peoples to Italy as forced workers in the fields, the court system turned to punitive enslavement as the chief form of punishment. In feudalism, when capitalism was still in its early moments, the scarcity of forms of value-exchange (money) meant that the easiest property to maintain was the serf's labour, which was legally due to the landlord, but not acquired through ownership in complete slavery, (the latter being increasingly costly and risky in times of disease epidemics that could kill slaves before they paid for their purchase with labour). In the first stages of a capitalist mercantile economy, labour begins to become a commodified product (labour-power) that is exchanged for wages. At this point, prisons begin to make inmates work in a prison factory as a testing ground for how workers can be exploited within a full-fledged capitalist economy. In later moments of a more developed capitalism, modern prison labour becomes less about exploiting value from the worker and more about 'correcting' a rebellious proletariat, weakening labour-class resistance to bourgeois rule.

Foucault does not immediately reject such a classical marxist approach. He says 'we can surely accept the general proposition' that punishment should be considered as part of the modern (capitalist) political economy, since the body's production of value (its 'utility') and the need to ensure the 'docility' of a passive workforce are key features of punishment (25). As we will later see, Foucault's definition of 'discipline' depends on the fusion of the need to make the body simultaneously more useful and docile. So if Foucault agrees with much of Rusche and Kirchheimer, what's his real disagreement?

Foucault says these earlier left sociologists did not consider the relationship of punishment to moral reform, the construction of the 'secret soul' of criminals (and everyone else). One of his book's particular contributions is the refusal to divide body and soul into two different aspects (another way in which Foucault challenges the tradition of the Enlightenment). In a larger sense, though, Foucault wants to understand why it is that we accept the forces that discipline us. The earlier left sociologists can explain the purely economic reasons why dominant social forces may use punishment in certain ways, but they do not explain why less empowered groups accept these actions as part of a supposedly neutral 'justice' system, rather than protesting against it as an obvious class tactic.

Conversely, Foucault can be said to be investigating the ways in which we consent to be ruled and punished. But he wants to avoid a simplistic model of ideological repression. He dislikes this explanation because it presents power as only negative in its actions. Foucault is wary of this since he sees it as part of the humanist and Enlightenment rhetoric, which he argues is equally complicit with discipline.

To complicate this perspective, Foucault then turns to the other side as he says that some historians have begun to consider the history of the socialized body as they write studies about the relationship of society to changes in population (demography) and sickness (pathology, desires, illness) and show that supposedly natural features of the body are socially and politically constructed, where certain kinds of illness, like the spread of tuberculosis, have a social explanation in the rise of the urban slums. Specifically mentioning the historian Emmanuel Le Roy Ladurie (1929–) (25), Foucault more generally refers to what was by then a long-standing, influential school of historical writing in France known as the *Annales* school, through their association with the journal *Annales d'histoire économique et sociale* (founded in 1929). The *Annalistes* were known for sidelining traditional historians' fascination with diplomatic, military and political history in favour of social, economic and cultural history; in that sense, Foucault, whose projects revolve around formerly marginalized identities (the criminal, the insane etc.) had much in common with them.

But Foucault disagrees with the *Annalistes* for how they seem to have given up too quickly on politics and marxist economics. For Foucault insists that the body is 'directly involved in a political field' (26) and the 'political investment of the body is bound up...with its economic use. It is largely as a force of production that the body is invested with relations of power and domination' (26–7). Foucault argues that the constitution and exploitation of labour-power (the exploitation of the proletariat) and creation of surplus-value for capitalist profit is 'possible only if it is caught up in a system of subjection' (26). In a theme that he will continually repeat, he says that bodies can only be useful if they are made to be productive (coerced and exploited labour) and subjected (made docile).

We can perceive now that Foucault sees himself as crafting an argument that is based neither in humanism nor solely within economics. In the paragraphs on Rusche and Kirchheimer and the newer social and cultural French history, Foucault strives to chart a third way, one that investigates the procedures of social domination within capitalist societies, while also exploring something as seemingly non-material as the rise of collective psychological outlooks or 'mentalities' to use a keyword for the *Annalistes*. The last pages of this section are Foucault's attempt to negotiate between his difference from both approaches, one relying too much on rational choice and intentionality as driving forces in history, the other seemingly lacking in human input.

Foucault insists that use of power can be premeditated, 'calculated, organized, technically thought out', but it does not have to deploy either 'weapons' or 'terror' even while it can 'remain of a physical order' (26). The soft coercion involved in the 'political technology of the body' is difficult to see, since it is 'rarely formulated in continuous, systemic discourse; it is often made up of bits and pieces' and draws together different tools and techniques (26). Because this form of power comes from different sources, it is a 'multiform instrumentation' and 'cannot be localized in a particular type of institution or state apparatus' (26). Foucault seems to be contrasting himself to the French marxist philosopher Louis Althusser (1918–1990), who defined social institutions, like education, as 'Ideological State Apparatuses'. For Foucault, it is not a macro-power, coming from forces above, such as the State, but a 'micro-physics of power', something that often works unseen, unrecognized and in the interstices of the agencies that we often recognize as constraining ourselves. It is also micro, since it works 'within' us and 'through' our bodies, rather than from the 'outside' as it were.

For this reason, Foucault offers some basic considerations about how to study the minute features of power that he is investigating. Firstly, power is not a 'property' of something or somebody else, but a 'strategy', a set of 'manoeuvres, tactics, techniques, functionings' that are chosen and used according to their efficacy (26). The source of this strategy, as of yet unnamed by Foucault, but implicitly the bourgeoisie, could have chosen or be forced to choose another means of power, since the 'network of relations' between social interests is 'constantly in tension, in activity, rather than a privilege' that lasts forever (26). Social forms are not produced as mechanically and homogenously as Rusche and Kirchheimer suggest. Power is not a thing, but a social process; it becomes manifested in changing forms because social relations are constantly in flux.

Secondly, power should not be thought of simply as a case of the haves dominating the have-nots; it is not something that one side unilaterally does to the other.

Neither is power a one-time conquest, a contract that once signed works forever. Instead it is the mobile result of the chess-like 'strategic positions' taken by those who constantly transmit, amplify, or resist power (26). Foucault does not imagine power relations being able to be simply divided between the classes or the State and the citizen; instead power works in a more complex fashion. The lines of power are often complicated because every group has its own subsets, all of which have their own particularities, affinities and antagonisms. This notion of power as a complex relation, rather than simple linear effect, is similar to Italian marxist Antonio Gramsci's (1891–1937) concept of 'hegemony', as a mixture of coercion and consent to any organization of society. When Foucault says that there is 'neither analogy nor homology, but a specificity of mechanism and modality' (27), he means to say that we cannot use the example of one set of relations, like that between the father and his children, as exactly similar to another, such as that between the State and its citizen. These power relations are not similar (analogous) or the same (homologous). Each one has its own specific way of operating depending on the particular tensions involved, even while sometimes two groups begin to mimic each other or take up another's tactics, an emulation that can be confused as both seem to represent the same interests. So while Foucault will make comparisons between how different social institutions operate, he is not looking to make a 'unified field theory' of fixed structure where everything can be compared to everything else in some universalizing or totalizing fashion. Instead, he wants to look at strategic alignments or coalitions of interests that are more fluid and sensitive to pressures, especially resistance from below.

Lastly, and similarly, Foucault emphasizes that these 'micro-powers' (27) are like a hydra. Because they have multiple points of contact, some might be defeated without damaging the general network. These micro-powers do not 'obey the law of all or nothing' (27). On the other hand, every 'localized episode[s]' anywhere in the network does have implications for the rest of it, since a local change might be the weak link that snaps that chain. Foucault is not interested in thinking about society as a fixed crystal, rather he imagines it as more inter-active, a network rather than a static structure.

With these cautions in mind, Foucault then repeats himself and encourages his readers to give up one of the basic tenets of the Enlightenment, which is that knowledge exists in the absence of power relations, that truth erodes and erases domination, and that we can 'speak truth to power' and overcome despotism by confronting it with reason, rational declarations and open communication. Foucault undercuts this notion by saying that modern forms of knowledge and modern forms of power are intertwined; one serves as the condition for the other's existence: 'there is no power relation without the correlative constitution of a field of knowledge, nor any knowledge that does not presuppose and constitute at the same time power relations' (27). Foucault uses the hyphenated 'power-knowledge' to indicate their intricate relationship. Rather than simply considering the relation of the empowered to the powerless, the free and the unfree, Foucault proposes a different model involving professional authorities ('the subject who knows'), humans who are classified through certain names and categories ('the objects to be known') and the institutional instruments that link the two ('the modalities of knowledge') (27–8).

This leads Foucault to sideline the familiar ways of analysing power such as an older model of marxism ('the violence-ideology opposition'), where it is assumed that one class simply physically and mentally dominates another; liberal political science and economy that imagines social exchanges as consensual and based on the exchange of commodities ('the metaphor of property, the model of the contract'); and scientificism that thinks we can analyse things without being caught up within power relations (that we can be 'disinterested') (28).

Instead Foucault argues for a 'political anatomy' of the 'body politic' that combines features of the mind and the body where 'human bodies' are 'subjugate[d] by turning them into objects of knowledge' (28). Here Foucault draws on an argument by the scholar of medieval Europe Ernst Kantorowicz's *The King's Two Bodies* (1957). Kantorowicz (1895–1963) argued that in regal society there was the actual king, but beyond the physical container that may have been a king, the concept of the King was 'virtual' and couldn't be damaged, even if the king was. Think of the slogan 'The King is dead; long live the King!' The phrase indicates that even though this king is dead, we still live in a monarchy; the regal institution transcends the individual.

Foucault argues that modernity has a different 'two body' system: our own physical body and the 'virtual' body, which is our psyche. Consider the popular claims that there is a difference between our biological 'sex' and the cultural way this physical difference is acted out, our 'gender'. We have biological sexual apparatus (genital difference), but there is also the concept that we have a sexuality that cannot be located simply in these genitals, since the cultural codes and socialization processes determine acceptable or conventional ways of behaviour depending on what biology one carries.

Foucault says that there is something similar to this symbolic virtualization with the condemned man, who creates a 'surplus power' (29) from his body, not only the surplus-value that arises from being exploited through unpaid labour, as traditional marxists would argue, but also from the institutional mechanism of punishment, which produces a surplus of its own, a 'non-corporal' aspect that is the 'soul'. Yet simply because the soul or spirit is intangible, it 'would be wrong to say that the soul is an illusion, or an ideological effect' (29). Foucault again distances himself from and complicates terms used in an older marxist tradition, such as 'ideology' and the claim that the economy alone is the 'base' that creates a fixed template that is mirrored or reflected in cultural and social 'superstructures', as a version of the body-mind split familiar from the Enlightenment. Foucault appears to complicate both. Although the soul 'is not a substance' itself, since it is a constructed or invented concept, it, nonetheless, has a material reality, as the concept is then grounded on the bodies of those it 'supervises, trains and corrects' (29): the insane, children, the colonized and the labouring class (interestingly, Foucault does not include the category of women here. While he occasionally mentions female criminals, he does not explicitly acknowledge gender difference as requiring further analysis). The soul becomes the object and reference point of knowledge production that, in turn, 'extends and reinforces the effects of [this] power' (29). From this relation, 'various concepts have been constructed... subjectivity, personality, consciousness' (29) that are often grounded on the claims of humanism. But Foucault warns us not to consider these as sites of freedom: 'The soul is the effect and instrument of a political anatomy; the soul is the prison of the body' (30).

You should also be aware of a problem in translation. In English we have one word – 'knowledge'. In French, there are two, *savoir* and *connaissance*, and these refer to different kinds of knowledge. *Savoir* is the kind of knowledge that is empirical, quantitative, rule- or skill-based and typically emerges from institutions, while *connaissance* is subjective, qualitative, situational and experiential. The difference might be that between saying 'I know Edinburgh is in Scotland' (this is *savoir*; I know a location in terms of a map defined by political geography) versus 'I know Edinburgh well' (this is *connaissance*; I know the city because I live here and have walked through it).

In *Discipline and Punish*, Foucault will always be examining *savoir*; knowledge which is 'made' or 'officiated' (produced as professional discourse) rather than individually or informally known. When he talks about 'power-knowledge', you might want to hear this as something akin to Marx's phrase of labour-power. While labour is something that everyone has and can do, labour-power only appears when individuals alienate their body's work power and sell their labour as a commodity on the marketplace (usually for wages). When Foucault is talking about knowledge and power, he seems to be referring to a particular mode of truth relations, a socially constructed (and implicitly disempowering) system of knowing things – and one that

Foucault implicitly wishes to challenge. Hopefully, this will become more self-evident as the book progresses.

Foucault concludes this chapter by turning to explain the immediate relevance of his study. He explains that he has learned that punishment and the prison 'belong to a political technology of the body...not so much from history as from the present' (30). Throughout the 1970s, most notably with the 1971 prison riot at the Attica Correctional Facility (New York State), uprisings in penitentiaries in the US and Europe brought prisoners' rights to the forefront. Foucault himself, throughout 1971 and 1972, was involved in *Le Groupe d'Information sur les Prisons* (GIP) [Prison Information Group], which sought to make visible the inner operations of France's prisons, to allow French prisoners' voices to be heard and protested the use of super high security prisons (*Quartiers de Haute Sécurité*) and prisoner isolation techniques. Foucault acknowledges that many of these revolts attacked the material conditions of prison's 'physical misery', but he also sees them as protests against the 'whole technology of power over the body' and the 'technology of the "soul"' provided by 'educationalists, psychologists and psychiatrists' (30). To this end, Foucault considers that his history of the prison and its 'political investments of the body' is not simply a matter of antiquarian interest in the past, but is also a 'history of the present', a history that wants to intervene in current social policies and politics by revealing the ways in which current society is constructed. The section ends with a footnote that says Foucault, for purposes of concision, will only use examples from France, but as suggested earlier in the section, the mechanisms and their development belong more generally to 'Western' nations.

2. The spectacle of the scaffold

After Foucault introduces his thesis, method and motive in the first section, he now begins his historical account proper. As we will see, Foucault roughly divides this historical narrative into three periods, which are remarkably accepting of the traditional ways of dividing French history. The first phase belongs to the early modern age after the downfall of Middle Ages feudalism; it runs roughly from the middle of the seventeenth century to the last third of the eighteenth century: from Louis XIV, the Sun King, to the last years of Louis XVI, dethroned by the French Revolution. The second phase, more or less, centres on the Revolutionary period, the years leading up to 1789 and ending with Napoleon's ascension to power. The final phase is the modern, nineteenth-century one from the post-Revolutionary moment when Napoleon becomes emperor in 1804 to the 1840s, with the rise to power of Louis-Napoleon, Napoleon's nephew. Although Foucault occasionally mentions later events, his historical examples very rarely go beyond the 1840s.

These three phases, roughly involving the *Ancien Régime* (ending in 1789), the Revolutionary Era (1789–99) and the Restoration to the start of the Second Empire (1799–1848/52), each correspond to the first three parts in *Discipline and Punish*, which are titled with their period's representative form of penality: torture, punishment and discipline. The final part, on prison, partly continues with the events of the third part and partly acts as Foucault's review and conclusion.

In the first part's first section, Foucault examines the early modern period's dominant form of punishment: torture and public displays of pain. Today a punishment intent on causing pain seems nearly unthinkable as a regular mode of punishment and a violation of basic human rights. Yet Foucault goes to lengths to show the logic of each penal form in its own historical environment. It is a tremendous mistake to think that, because we exist within a later historical moment, our society is somehow 'smarter' than prior ones or that we live in a more advanced ethics, according to Foucault. Much of *Discipline and Punish* is dedicated to rejecting this notion of development, arguing instead that each historical phase organizes itself in ways that make sense for its particular dominant mode of sociopolitical organization. Later phases are not better than earlier ones; they are just organized differently.

To show this, Foucault tends to organize each of his parts and sections with an unsaid, but consistent structure. He usually begins each part by defining the end marks of the phase it covers and goes on to describe the period's techniques (or technologies) of punishment. He then characterizes the ways in which the body is used within these techniques and concludes by discussing the politics surrounding the organization of penal forms of embodiment: each phase's unique 'political technology of the body'.

Consequently, this section begins by characterizing the 'general forms of penal practice' (32) defined by the Ordinance of 1670. This French code of criminal law was introduced in the early years of Louis XIV's adult rule and remained in effect until 1789, the first year of the French Revolution. Beginning the section in this way, Foucault makes clear that he is dealing with the pre-Revolutionary phase that is associated with the rise of Absolutism, the post-feudal centralization of power by the monarch at the expense of other nobles. This period of the absolutist monarch is not pre-modern so much as it is early modern, belonging to the period between feudalism, the time of weak kings whose rule was fragile against the power of local nobles/warlords, and the late Enlightenment, the time when rule by all shades of aristocratic and religious elites was challenged by a rising middle class.

The main feature of the absolutist monarch's penal practice involves sentences of physical pain. While the death penalty was often prescribed for a host of crimes, Foucault notes that the courts, in actual practice, often found ways to mitigate the death sentence and substitute it with other kinds of punishment, either by refusing to prosecute crimes that were 'too heavily punished' or by changing the 'definition of the crime' that an individual was accused of committing (33). Although the death sentence was not as common in real practice as might be imagined if one only read the written legal codes, punishment, nevertheless, mainly 'involved a degree of torture: public exhibition, pillory, carcan [iron collaring], flogging, branding', in short, *supplice*, which Foucault says is '[c]orporal punishment, painful to a more or less horrible degree' (33).

The period's torture was not, however, random or without a kind of logic informing its use. 'Torture is a technique; it is not an extreme expression of lawless rage' (33). For torture to be a legitimate part of the legal apparatus in the *Ancien Régime*, it had to 'obey three principal criteria' (33). It must produce pain that can be 'measured exactly, or at least calculated, compared and hierarchized' (33). Human sensation must have a kind of mathematical scale to its use, thus rationalizing it to some degree. Secondly, it must be possible to regulate the 'quality, intensity, duration of pain' (34) through these measurements so as to be able to deliver the appropriate amount of pain for different kinds of crime. Thirdly, torture must be part of a ritual that produces both the truth of the crime (by means of a confession) as well as its punishment. This knowledge-producing ritual has two aspects: it must 'mark the victim' (torture must leave a physical trace behind in the form of a scar, brand, or disfigurement, so that the flesh acts as a permanent record of punishment) and it must be displayed in public exhibition, hence the section's title: 'spectacle of the scaffold'. The excessive visual display of torture is one of punishment's purposes; the cries of pain by the criminal are 'not a shameful side-effect, it is the very ceremonial of justice being expressed in all its force' (34).

The phase's 'penal torture', therefore, is not simply corporal punishment: it combines three key elements: 'a differentiated production of pain, an organized ritual for the marking of victims and the expression of the power that punishes' (34). Torture's circus does not emerge from a legal system that has forgotten human principles and restraint. Instead, justice's 'economy of power' *depends* on producing these 'excesses' through torture, since the purpose of public torture is to make 'open for all to see, the truth of the crime' (35).

With the exception of England, most European countries kept the trial's procedure of determining guilt private, away from the public, and a secret even to the accused, who would not be told what crime he or she was accused of committing, the nature of the evidence or identity of witnesses against him or her. The accused individual was not usually allowed to have a lawyer, to speak on his or her own behalf, or even be sure if the judge's questions were merely intended to confuse and trick him or her into a self-incrimination or accidental confession. The person was simply interrogated and then judged. The magistrate had 'solitary omnipotence' (35) or complete power to determine guilt and sentencing. 'The secret and written form of the procedure reflects the principle that in criminal matters the establishment of truth was the absolute right and the exclusive power of the sovereign and his judges' (35). These courts were distanced from the public's eye because authorities were concerned that having an audience might create an uproar of protest during the trial. In matters of justice, the 'multitude' (36), or common people, had no say, since this was not a democratic society, but one ruled over by an absolute monarch, a sovereign, whose power was based on the King's supposedly divine right to rule, not one granted to him by a democratic public election or approbation.

Even if the trial done in the King's name was secret, 'certain rules had to be obeyed in establishing the truth' (36). These rules involved a penal 'arithmetic' (37) where half-proofs could be added up to produce a complete one, and circumstantial evidence could be piled on to deliver guilt conclusively. Yet because there was still some doubt by the period's legal commentators about a system that gave the judge so much power to determine the truth of a crime, the trial had to work in ways that helped to legitimize its activity. The 'penal investigation' had to be 'a machine that might produce the truth' (37), and this truth was ultimately defined by the need for torture to produce a confession by the accused.

The confession became important for two reasons. Firstly, the confession was highlighted because it was considered to be the strongest proof, par excellence, of crime. A confession did not even require the presence of any other evidence at all. Secondly, the legitimacy of penal authority was achieved when 'the accused himself took part in the ritual of producing penal truth' and confirmed his or her own accusation by coming to 'play the role of living truth' (38). The prisoner's oral statement authenticated and complemented the court's written accusations. If the confession was both an 'element of proof and the counterpart of the preliminary investigation', it had the result of making the torture seem like a 'semi-voluntary transaction' (39). Consequently, Foucault says, it makes sense that the prisoner's oath against perjury was so central to the process of producing the truth of a subject's guilt that this oath had to be repeated 'spontaneous[ly]' a second time after the torture was over in order to demonstrate that the confession was real and voluntarily given (39).

While Enlightenment thinkers would accuse the *Ancien Régime* and compare its use of torture to feudalism's gothic behaviour and its perverse inquisitions as similar to the cruelty of ancient slave-holding societies, Foucault argues that the pre-Enlightenment, early modern period did not simply reproduce older customs; it reconfigured older methods of torture for its own needs. The period of the absolutist monarch had its own rational-looking regulations, in which the procedures of the inquisition were modified by the inclusion of new elements, like the need for the convergence of written accusations and the prisoner's oral confessions and for the confession to be a 'voluntary' act, where the accused participated ('if necessary by the most violent persuasion') in their own condemnation (39).

The reason for this regulation about torture, which was absent in feudalism, is political. Because the central authority of the King was itself a relatively new system of government, even the absolutist state had to make its use of power logical and acceptable to its subjects. Consequently, the period's mechanism of producing truth had two elements: a secret investigation by a judge and a public enactment 'ritually performed by the accused' (39). The third aspect that linked the two elements together was the 'body of the accused, the speaking and, if necessary, suffering body' (40) that was then displayed in public as a means of justifying the unseen trial and its sentence.

Because the accused body's shrieks were necessary to certify and legitimize the production of juridical truth, the period's commentators were very concerned to ensure that torture functioned properly and without error. Torture was 'certainly cruel but it was not savage' for it had to exist within certain parameters; mathematical gradations to painful torture made it 'a regulated practice, obeying a well-defined procedure' (40). Yet because the need for a confession to validate the accusation was so great, a paradox arose. If the prisoner did not confess after torture, the 'magistrate was forced to drop the charges' (41), since the most valid form of evidence failed to appear. Although the judge seemed to have all the power, he could be overcome in the 'ordeal' of torture. Juridical torture was 'a way of obtaining evidence... but it was also the battle...that "produced" truth... there was an element of the duel' (41). To get around this possible loophole, magistrates often changed the wording of their accusations so that a non-confession did not prove a person's innocence, but saved her or him from receiving the death penalty. In this way, officials would not have to declare the accused entirely innocent simply because they could not obtain a confession.

As the eighteenth century approached, this mixed nature of torture – 'investigation and punishment' – was found to be confusing and objectionable (41). But for the period just before the Revolution, the public display of torture and confession was necessary for four reasons. Firstly, it acted as a means of legitimizing the authority to judge by making the guilty man 'the herald of his own condemnation' (43). Secondly, it repeated 'the scene of the confession' (43) before the public which had otherwise been prohibited from witnessing the process of determining guilt; it added the 'signature of the convicted man' (44) to reveal what had previously been a private truth. The latter is why public executions often combined aspects of the trial, where the accused could make new confessions on the scaffold and also denounce others. Thirdly, the spectacle of punishment worked to pin responsibility for 'the public torture on to the crime itself' (44), rather than the judge, thus absolving justice authorities. Consequently, there was the effort to have the public punishment occur near the scene of the crime, as if the proximity of event to punishment could remove the intervening presence of juridical authorities.

Lastly, the tempo of the public punishment was often slowed down on the scaffold as a device to make the confession's 'ultimate proof' (45) gain in intensity for the viewing crowd. Punishment's theatricality was amplified by slowing its pace and by allowing spectators to watch and listen in slow motion, as it were. This carefully orchestrated process constituted, as Foucault, quoting the Italian jurist Giambattista Vico (1668–1744) notes, '"an entire poetics"' (45). The public torture and execution, with the body in pain at its centre, 'constituted a sign' to be read by the watching public (46). Foucault emphasizes the 'ambiguity'

How to Read Foucault's *Discipline and Punish*

of this poetics in that the convict's suffering 'may signify equally well the truth of the crime or the error of the judges, the goodness or the evil of the criminal, the coincidence or the divergence between the judgment of men and that of God' (46). Foucault repeatedly stresses the key role of punishment on the body, since 'the body, several times tortured, provides the synthesis of the reality of the deeds and the truth of the investigation, of the documents of the case and the statements of the criminal, of the crime and the punishment' (47).

Having explained the techniques and logic of the body in relation to truth creation, Foucault returns to explain its role 'not only as a judicial, but also as a political ritual' (47). Within a society organized by the centralization of power, crime is mainly perceived as an act of rebellion against the system of government represented by the sovereign. Because the King is the source of justice, any violation of the legal code, that is to say, any crime, 'attacks the sovereign: it attacks him personally, since the law represents the will of the sovereign; it attacks him physically, since the force of the law is the force of the prince' (47).

Consequently, regardless of the crime's actual victim, the King stands as its symbolic target, since the monarch is the source of the law's authority. Because any crime is thus an act of insubordination to his rule, the King must be seen as personally taking revenge. Consequently, the public execution is 'a ceremonial by which a momentarily injured sovereignty is reconstituted' (48). The King's power includes the right to punish the criminal in much the same way as the King has the 'right to make war on his enemies' (48). And lest the authority of the sovereign be further challenged, any attack on the King must be met not only with a victorious force, but a 'super-power'; an overwhelming display of power that will terrorize anyone else who might think to challenge the sovereign.

Hence the public execution is conducted much as if it were a military victory parade, a spectacular display of the King's 'invincible force' (48), where the purpose is not merely to redress the wound, but to enact overwhelming revenge. Like the example of Damiens shows, there must be a disproportionate penality as 'an emphatic affirmation of [the King's] power and of its intrinsic superiority... [t]he ceremony of punishment, then, is an exercise of "terror"...to make everyone aware, through the body of the criminal, of the unrestrained presence of the sovereign' (49). The public execution's ruthless spectacle and physical violence orchestrated within a ceremony is, therefore, a key explanation of the 'political functioning of the penal system' (49), whereby the watching crowd must itself be terrorized by the display of the tortured criminal.

The public execution's shock and awe was created through the theatrical pomp of the criminal's procession through the crowd and ensuing gestures of expiation. These events were often accompanied by military guards (the 'armed justice') who were present partially 'to prevent any outbursts of sympathy or anger on the part of the people' or attempt to save the criminal, but 'it was also a reminder that every crime constituted as it were a rebellion against the law and that the criminal was an enemy of the prince' (50). The King, as the 'head of justice and head of war' (50) presided over a great asymmetry of power and turned the public execution into a sort of jousting between the King and the criminal, where the criminal must always submit to the monarch's power (it did not even matter if the King pardoned the criminal at the last minute, so long as it was made clear that all power resided in the monarch's decision on whether or not to take life). The wrathful sovereign's force (through his agents) was therefore 'at' every execution. The sovereign 'directly or indirectly, demanded, decided and carried out punishments' since 'it was he who, through the law, had been injured by the crime' (53).

Foucault now returns to mention Rusche and Kirchheimer's study, since he recognizes that his claim about the relationship between the absolutist sovereign and torture's disregard for the body is close to their argument that this kind of punishment exists in a time of weakly developed capitalism, a time with 'a system of production in which labour power, and therefore the human body, has neither the utility nor the commercial value that are conferred on them in an economy of an industrial type' (54) and can be thus easily 'wasted' without concern. Foucault likewise acknowledges that the acceptability of torture displays might have been higher at a time in Europe when death was often a frequent occurrence, due to epidemic plagues and scarcity of food (an *Annaliste*-type point). But neither explanation is completely convincing to Foucault, since the late seventeenth century/early eighteenth century had a more developed form of mercantile capitalism than Rusche and Kirchheimer allowed and it was later than the great plagues. Similarly, these two explanations cannot account for why the Ordinance of 1670, which is the main legal code for this time, often made punishments harsher than they were in earlier ones.

Foucault instead sees this new severity as a response to the fragility of the institution of monarchy. France had just experienced a civil war, called the Fronde (1648–53), during a period when Louis XIV was technically king, but as a child monarch, one with uncertain power. When Louis came of age after the military defeat of the noble insurgents, he put new, more severe laws into effect. There are, therefore, clearly strategic reasons for the public execution's 'ruthlessness, its spectacle, its physical violence' (49) having to do with the need for the monarch to reestablish his supreme authority at a socially turbulent moment: '[at] the rumbling close at hand of civil war, the king's desire to assert his power at the expense of the parlements go[es] a long way to explain the survival of so severe a penal system' (55).

Foucault also recounts the aspects inherent in the spectacle of the scaffold and how they combined different features: the written and the oral; the private secret and public display; the procedure of the investigation and the confession's validation of the inquiry; the crime and its visible reproduction on the criminal's body, where the flesh's disfigurement symbolically replaced and annulled the crime's disturbance. These oppositions become fused on the scaffold, which was an 'anchoring point' for the 'manifestation of power' by a vengeful sovereign (55), as if to assert that it is within the aura of the King that all social elements become best expressed and maintained.

Enlightenment figures would shortly afterward condemn public torture as an act of atrocity, but they would not ask or explain the tactical purpose these acts had for the King: the need for punishment that would meet and overcome the 'atrocity' of crime that was considered a violent challenge to the sovereign's authority. The purpose of spectacular punishment was precisely to stand as a 'ritual destruction of infamy by omnipotence' (57), a monarchical 'super-power' that would brook no form of dissent.

The main audience for the public execution's spectacle was not the King's aristocratic competitors, the nobility, but the commoners, the 'people'. The monarch depended on the common people for revenue-creating labour to pay for the armies that he required to compete against the other nobles' armies. The public is summoned to the execution to both witness and participate in its terror, so that commoners are brought into direct contact and union with the King's terrifying authority, rather than through the intermediaries of the Church or other aristocrats. Yet while the crowd's activity in the execution was meant to consolidate frightened allegiance to the King and bind the people to the monarch rather than their local gentry or priest, the opposite could also happen when crowds rioted to defend the criminal, rather than attack him or her. Authorities accepted some crowd violence at executions, if it was directed at the criminal, since this was seen as a symbolic gesture wherein the people could play 'an unobtrusive part' in the 'vengeance of the sovereign' (59). Crowd unrest was read as the people showing their allegiance to the King, but within limits set by the monarch's own privileges and, of course, the military guards present at the scaffold.

Yet in the years of food shortages preceding the Revolution, crowds increasingly refused to act in expected ways: these public events became moments that could magnetize popular resistance and a carnival-like refusal to respect the monarch's authority. Sometimes the crowd would riot against authorities if they felt that the sentence was unfairly harsh on non-elite figures for committing small crimes. In these years, a new solidarity emerged where the labouring classes began to align themselves with petty offenders, like 'vagrants, false beggars, the indigent poor, pickpockets, receivers and dealers in stolen goods' (63) that the lower classes would otherwise look to the police to prosecute. In the years leading up to the Revolution, there was more collusion between the 'honest' poor and the criminal underclass, as the former would help the latter resist police searches and informers. If the military usually accompanied the criminal to the scaffold, it was increasingly less as a spectacular display of the State's authority and more as a necessary armed defence against the possible outburst of popular unrest.

When crowds were restive at executions, they symbolically resisted the legitimacy of the King himself, and this caused a 'political fear' (65) for authorities, who saw their own techniques turned against them. For instance, the ritual of the 'gallows speech', the purported last words of the criminal, was meant to authenticate the punishment, but it then also became a tool for criminals to condemn their punishers. This allowed the shortly-to-be-killed criminal to become something of a spokesperson and martyred hero for the poor. The gallows speech of anger or resistance to elites could ventriloquize a 'whole memory of struggles and confrontations' (67) between the lower classes and their rulers, so crowds often came to executions precisely to hear 'an individual who had nothing more to lose curse the judges, the laws, the government and religion' (60). The proclamation of the accused's 'crimes blew up to epic proportions the tiny struggle that passed unperceived in everyday life' (67) and helped the lower classes build up a proto-political language of complaint in a time when these groups did not (yet) have either freedom of speech or the means to overthrow those that governed them. While the broadsheets publicizing the criminal's complaints should not be read as 'a spontaneous form of "popular expression"' (67), their popularity can be seen as reflecting the desire of the lower ranks to participate in a scene of confrontation with the authorities. Hence the people often turned the criminal into a 'positive hero' and 'a sort of saint' (67) that allegorically acted in their interests, a sort of Robin Hood against the government.

As Foucault notes, existing records make it difficult to gauge whether these gallows speeches, typically printed on broadsheets, had actually been delivered or not (65–6). But he also implies that regardless of its authenticity, this literature of crime fulfilled an important social function, acting as 'a sort of battleground around the crime, its punishment and its memory' (67). Foucault suggests that these texts are best understood as 'two-sided discourses' which simultaneously 'justified justice, but also glorified the criminal' (68). This ambiguity, with its subversive potential of heroizing criminals, was one reason why penal reformers called for a ban on the literature of the scaffold.

In a similar move, Foucault argues that middle-class intellectuals would later condemn terror and torture as inhuman because they knew that it was safe to do so, since the torture system had already been discredited by the lower, plebeian classes, who were no longer frightened by the terror of public executions. The implication within Foucault's claim here is that it is the lower classes that make actual social change, while the middle classes take credit for it. Consequently, Foucault's examples of popular resistance are from the 1770s, the period before the official start of the Revolution, during which middle-class politicians would put Louis XVI on trial and then execute him in public. Foucault suggests that one reason why the middle class might have participated in this execution may have been to preempt even more radical action by the lower classes; the execution of Louis XVI operated as a means of calibrating popular anger by controlling the people's desire for revenge on past rulers.

Foucault ends this section with one other, cultural example of how the middle class goes to lengths to try to recontain popular expressions of dissent as the period's (middle-class) reformers began to suppress the older broadsheets of the criminal's last speech and instead developed a 'whole new literature of crime...in which crime is glorified, because it is one of the fine arts, because it can be the work only of exceptional natures...[where] villainy is yet another mode of privilege' (68). The purpose of this new 'aesthetic of crime' is to make it seem as if crime is something that the lower classes are not intelligent or sophisticated enough to commit, and when this criminal is met by his or her double, the detective, and vanquished, he or she is not tortured. Both crime and its defeat now become the 'exclusive privilege' of the middle class. 'The literature of crime transposes to another social class the spectacle that had surrounded the criminal' so that 'the people was robbed of its old pride in its crimes; the great murders had become the quiet game of the well behaved' (69).

This anecdote of how the middle class uses a new mode of representation to gain social influence acts as Foucault's transition to the next phase of punishment.

Part Two: Punishment

Perhaps no other chapter of *Discipline and Punish* has received as little care in its reading as the second part. This part depicts the characteristics of the intervening historical phase between the *Ancien Régime*'s terror, just described, and the modern one of discipline, which will be treated in Part Three. This middle phase mainly involves the period leading up to and including the French Revolution until roughly Napoleon's rise around 1800. Because this period is sandwiched in between two longer phases, as a transitional time, readers have often overlooked it to read *Discipline and Punish* as a 'big ditch' book, one that sets up a clear break between a 'pre-'modern period and the modern one. In fact, Foucault is careful to show the reverse by indicating his history is one of multiple shifts and transformations.

Foucault, however, shares some blame for how Part Two easily recedes in readers' memory. Partly because he generally wants to downplay the role of enlightened human-itarianism as a progressive cause, he spends less time on it. Similarly, he does not directly acknowledge the effect of the French Revolution, only referring in passing to some dates or laws within it. As noted in our Rationale, at the start of this book, he is relatively silent on the Revolution because the history of the French Revolution is a hotly contested specialty within France. Foucault wants to carve his own relationship to Marx's writing on capitalist economies and to give him the clear grounds to do so, he tends, throughout his career, to simply avoid any discussion of the Revolutionary 1790s that might entangle him with the positions of other historians. Finally, because the role of Enlightenment intellectuals (*philosophes*) and the events of the Revolution are part of most French schoolchildren's historical education, Foucault assumes that only a brief word or allusion is necessary for his readers to understand his argument. English readers tend to be less familiar with this history and so the second part's language can seem vague or overly abstract to its readers.

As mentioned, Foucault tends to follow a threefold argument about the 'political technology of the body'. He first details a historical phase's particular penal techniques and their own form of truth-power, then follows this with a discussion of their combined impact on the body and concludes by explaining the political strategy for the above. In Part Two, he follows this order, but separates it into two sections. The first mainly treats the first aspect and the second carries out the latter two.

1. Generalized punishment

Foucault indicates a new phase of treating criminals as he begins this section with an example of a petition against torture and executions from 1789, the year that is conventionally taken as the start of the French Revolution. Foucault describes how protest against public executions (the terror system) 'proliferated in the second half of the eighteenth century' by a range of Enlightenment *philosophes*, middle-class lawyers, parliamentarians from the lower ranks

How to Read Foucault's *Discipline and Punish*

of the aristocracy and popular petitions (73). These groups complained that the old system was too violent and insisted that a new, less brutal form of punishment be created. Foucault, however, argues that the initial anxiety driving complaints about public executions was that the terrifying spectacle brought together and amplified a potentially uncontrollable force as the 'vengeance of the prince and the contained anger of the people' (73) converged on one space. The double violence of the King and the violence of the people might mutually enable each other to create a new force which it might be impossible to control, a fear that the Revolution would prove potentially very real. As '[regal] tyranny confronts [popular] rebellion; each calls forth the other' (74), for once the public became accustomed to seeing blood flow by the King, it might want to do this for itself.

To prevent this fusion of regal and popular violence, criminal justice had to stop staging moments where the criminal would suffer 'revenge'. Instead there were calls for 'punishment' to lack any bloody drama. Foucault argues that the rejection of torture was initially less a humanitarian desire than a means by which humanitarian concerns could be used as a tactic. This tactic allowed bourgeois-led groups (the Third Estate that were neither nobles, nor priests) to justify limits on the monarch's power by rejecting the King's right to touch (or maim) the body of his subjects. Foucault says that the attempt to limit the King's power came before the rhetoric of 'humanitarian' sentiment. In other words, a concern for anti-regal politics preceded ethics; the middle class wanted to resist the King and needed a (self) justifying language, which was the language of humanitarianism.

Likewise, these reformers cloaked their concerns about lower-class revolt within a 'humanitarian' language about bodily pain. This rhetoric lays the roots for the later nine-teenth-century claim that justice should not only *not* destroy the criminal, but try to correct and transform him or her. Here Foucault is also setting up a later argument in the book by illustrating that the foundations of 'criminological' sciences and 'penitentiary' practices (74) are based in a concern to control the labouring and poor classes. However, in the late eighteenth century, the modern techniques of punishment, which Foucault will call 'discipline', remained to be fully created and consolidated. In their absence, most eighteenth-century writings about penality initially limited their concern to calls for the end of external forms of bodily pain on prisoners, as a means of limiting monarchical power. The criminal's newly emphasized humanity became a measure of power.

In this light, Foucault rhetorically asks how 'man-measure' came to emerge as a new concern for reformers. The allusion here is slightly awkward for English speakers. In one sense, Foucault is here silently drawing on a classic text of the materialist Enlightenment, *L'homme machine* [Man-the-Machine] published in 1748 by Julien Offray de La Mettrie (1709–1751) to represent a whole tradition of late humanism that places the individual human as the secular centre of reference and authority, the source of intrinsic human *rights*, rather than *liberties* that are granted to subjects by external forces, like the monarch. In another sense, Foucault uses de La Mettrie, because he wants to emphasize the conjunction between 'measurement' and 'humanity' that will be 'articulated upon one another, in a single strategy' (74) of social science discourse, rather than satirical reason or supercharged sentimentality represented by other Enlightenment figures like Voltaire or Rousseau.

Typically, we think of scientific measures and objective standards as the opposite of human relations. After all, it is a cliché of the post-Romantic era that the arts and sciences are supposed to be enemies. Foucault instead argues that before science saw itself as empirical and rationally argued and left it to the arts to define what it means to be human, the two were mutually intertwined in ways that became expressed with the rise of the social sciences as a hybrid form of anthropological knowledge. Furthermore, the early links between the sciences and the arts became the means by which the older regime of punishment was effectively construed as obsolete and inferior.

So while traditional accounts give homage to the great writers on prison reform, like Beccaria and the others listed on page 75, Foucault argues that it is a mistake to take the Enlightenment's intellectuals at their word and believe that their supposedly class-interest-free, rational arguments carried the day. Foucault instead encourages us to look at the historical archive to explain the tactics shaping changing social relations.

For instance, he points out that there was a shift in the nature and kind of crime as time went on. While crimes in the seventeenth century were often violent and conducted in large groups, the eighteenth century saw crimes that were less likely to be ones of 'physical acts of aggression' (75), like murder and assault, and more ones against property, like theft and swindling. As the latter were commonly committed by smaller groups or individuals, there was also a shift from 'mass criminality', involving attacks on bodies, to a 'marginal criminality', involving 'the more or less direct seizure of goods' (76). If crime became less violent as time went on, it became easier, Foucault implies, to argue that punishment should also become less violent. Conversely, Foucault suggests at points that the 'terror' system tends to return in times of greater popular unrest and rebellion.

Yet it is not just simply that harsh punishment was not as necessary as crime became less violent. Foucault explains the shift away from terror as part of 'a whole complex mechanism' (77) involving changing social conditions and economic pressures throughout the eighteenth century. These transformations mainly involved 'an increase in wealth and property' (76) as some farmers and an emerging commercial, urban middle class became wealthier and there was a sudden growth in population and longevity from the mid eighteenth century onward ('a large demographic expansion', 76). As there were literally more people around than before, the lower classes experienced falling wages, due to increased competition for work, and they found it harder to secure basic food and housing. The resulting inequality between nascent (rural and urban) capitalists and (rural and urban) workers resulted in the rise of a floating population of vagabonds. As peasants left or were forced off their traditional farming plots and poor city-dwellers found it difficult to secure stable work, both groups often left their home regions and became floating, landless individuals depending on theft to survive.

Foucault summarizes this turn from a 'criminality of blood to a criminality of fraud' (77) as driven by a rising mode of (capitalist) production, increase in wealth for the class reaping the benefits of that production and a greater value placed on 'property relations' (rather than the ones of customary deference to the local lord or priest). The rising groups, which we lump under the name of the middle class, then insisted that criminal justice focus on smaller crimes, like stealing, which the *Ancien Régime* had ignored, and called for a new police network to create surveillance techniques that paid more attention to the movement of the lower classes as a means of ensuring 'security' by isolating the population into ever smaller groups and seeking to gain more information about individuals than previously.

We might like to think that the shift towards leniency in punishment was a change in mentality towards a humanitarian concern for people, but Foucault insists that the 'shift in illegal practices' towards crimes against property was the driving force behind the 'refinement of punitive practices (77). 'What was emerging no doubt was not so much a new respect for the humanity of the condemned' (since torture continued to exist), but 'a tendency towards a more finely tuned justice, towards a closer penal mapping of the social body' (78), where people's 'everyday behaviour, their identity, their activity, their apparently unimportant gestures' were placed under tighter surveillance (77). While crimes became less violent, the forces of the police became more present and interventionist. Police surveillance of the public was driven by the desire to protect property, even while it used a rhetoric of public safety and care for humans in the abstract as its justification for new methods of social control.

This new form of policing had the 'bourgeois appearances of a class justice' (76), Foucault says, citing the *Annaliste* historian Emmanuel Le Roy Ladurie again, as the justice system became reorganized to service the needs of a rising capitalist market economy. The change in penality was driven by the desires of the middle class and the thinkers associated with it to fashion a mechanism that could control the 'multiplicity of bodies and forces that constitutes a population' (77–8), a means for breaking up the new flows and movements of the labouring classes that came about as a result of the nascent capitalist fragmentation of the *Ancien Régime*.

Furthermore, this move towards the protection of property *precedes* the events of the French Revolution. Foucault implies that the middle class began to change French society even before the Revolution; so if he shies away from attributing social change to great dates and events and more towards a history of smaller, harder to discern events, it is because he feels that these monumental events miss the real start of historical changes. Additionally, Foucault dissents from the view that the shift to more lenient forms of punishment is a '"change that belongs to the domain of the spirit and the subconscious"' (77). Although he cites a Sorbonne doctoral thesis by Nels Wayne Mogensen for the phrase, which hearkens back to a Hegelian or Freudian history of ideas, Foucault's target seems to be the *Annaliste* interest in charting mentalities or shifts on outlook over time. Foucault's point here is that historical change occurs due to strategic adjustments of the 'mechanisms of power' (77), not simply preconscious or quasi-supernatural forces.

Though Foucault does not turn his discussion towards this question, it might be worth considering a counter-factual or alternative case history. If modern punishment has its roots with the rise of the middle-class and the capitalist marketplace, then would we have a different penal justice system if our society were not one dominated and organized by middle-class concerns? Would a non- or post-capitalist society organize its justice system differently?

The question of the counter-factual is also important for our larger attitude towards *Discipline and Punish*. Many readers of the work, who ignore the historical argument, experience it as ultimately a bleak vision of modern life without any escape. As we will see, it is hard to reconcile this tragic world-view with either Foucault's motivation or the actual argument in the book, which locates 'discipline' in a particular historical moment that, Foucault implies, will eventually be substituted by new social formations.

In explaining the shift to 'a refinement of punitive practices' (77), Foucault now argues that penal reformers had three main socioeconomic complaints about what they say was unfair or un-'natural' about the *Ancien Régime*'s justice system. Firstly, hereditary judgeships were increasingly sold as commodities to individuals so that the judges who purchased their posts had to recover their investment by increasing court costs and fines, both of which made it more expensive for the middle class to use the court system. Secondly, there was a contradiction between the King being allowed to make laws that he was not held accountable for obeying, giving him an 'irrational' position as a force outside or above the law. Because there was no bureaucratic check on the monarch, he was a 'super-power' above the law, a position felt to be 'irregular' and 'unnatural' to the classes looking to make predictable what was legal or not (78–80). Finally, the King complicated the order of the legal system by selling 'offices of judges' as a means of raising revenue. The result was a nest of overlapping jurisdictions, a 'multiplicity of courts' that did not form 'a single and continuous pyramid' of appeals (78). These confusions of precedence and discontinuities 'left penal justice with innumerable loopholes' (79) that weakened its authority and ability to act decisively. This indeterminacy bothered the middle class who wanted some assurance that if one court ruled in their favour, the ruling would not be overturned or expensively recontested in another.

Foucault claims that prison reformers were thus more concerned with fixing a 'bad economy of power' rather than making it less cruel (79).

> The true objective of the reform movement, even in its most general formulations, was not so much to establish a new right to punish based on more equitable principles, as to set up a new 'economy' of the power to punish, to assure its better distribution, so that it should be neither too concentrated at certain privilege points, nor too divided between opposing authorities; so that it should be distributed in homogeneous circuits capable of operating everywhere, in a continuous way, down to the finest grain of the social body. (80)

Doing so would increase the effects of justice, while lowering its economic costs (caused by the selling of offices and its ensuing corruption) and the political cost of the justice system being associated with the unpopular monarchy. 'In short, the power to judge should no longer depend on the innumerable, discontinuous, sometimes contradictory privileges of sovereignty, but on the continuously distributed effects of public power' (81).

It was a need for a more rationalized 'political economy' of punishment that was paramount. Rather than offering a reductionist or simplistic account, Foucault is careful to note that there was a 'remarkable strategic coincidence', with 'many different interests' (81) converging and making way for social change. Instead of attributing importance to the writers of prison reform, Foucault says that it was not, above all, the intellectuals 'who regarded themselves as enemies of despotism and friends of mankind' who drove prison reform (81). The more important players were lawyers and magistrates, those *within* the system who were frustrated by their lack of control.

Consequently, Foucault argues that the language of 'reform' was less motivated by 'a new sensibility' of humanitarianism, than by 'another policy with regard to illegalities' (82). The motivation was 'not to punish less, but to punish better' in order to 'insert the power to punish more deeply into the social body' (82). Sometimes certain laws were not obeyed because later laws changed earlier ones, thus legitimizing certain kinds of activity. Sometimes older laws were either massively ignored or had, more or less, just been forgotten. The main reason, though, for inconsistencies in upholding the laws, was that the authorities did not seriously try to pursue or stop certain illegal acts.

Within the *Ancien Régime*, 'different social strata' had aspects of 'tolerated illegality' (82), acts that were technically illegal but were often carried out without fear or expectation of punishment, since these illegalities were either ignored or allowed to occur so long as this did not challenge the structure of social hierarchy. A modern-day example of tolerated illegality might be when an office manager does nothing when she or he knows that employees are taking office supplies, like pens, home with them. While tacit illegality is common in all kinds of societies, Foucault argues that it had become so 'deeply rooted and so necessary' (82) to the *Ancien Régime*'s operation that it became a structural feature of its coherence. These customary practices of soft criminality were especially necessary for the lower classes and small farmers. While they did not have many legal 'privileges', or things they could demand from their superiors, they did have a 'space of tolerance' (82) for slightly illegal activities (like smuggling, poaching, collecting wood for heating from the local manor's forest or squatting and farming on land they did not own).

These *Ancien Régime* illegalities were allowed to occur unchecked because they would have been either very difficult (if not impossible) to police or any effort to force the law back into life would have been met with 'popular disturbances', since these illegalities were 'so indispensible a condition of existence' (82). A contemporary example of tolerated illegality in this way is the presence of the 'black' market in goods, which is lightly policed since it provides a mechanism for commerce in sometimes essential goods that the official channels cannot provide, such as providing painkillers to people who might not otherwise be able to afford a visit to the doctor authorized to write the prescription.

This 'necessary illegality' (83) had certain intrinsic paradoxes, however. Firstly, it was often difficult for authorities to 'mark the frontiers' (83) and distinguish petty illegalities from more substantive criminality. When should vagabondage be allowed as a safety valve for the unemployed or for those who had been mistreated as servants or soldiers in search of better life conditions and when was it a real threat to have strange individuals floating around the countryside? This ambiguity also existed for the lower classes that both glorified and blamed, alternatively helped and feared, the 'shifting population' (83) of people thrown into movement by the changes of the eighteenth century. Peasants looked favourably at rural labourers who had escaped their abusive master and become criminals or smugglers, bringing untaxed goods more cheaply to the lower classes, but people who committed crimes against them 'became the object of a special hate' (83).

Also, one social group was initially encouraged by a second group to engage in certain kinds of illegal activity, in order to undermine a third. More clearly, local landowners did not mind when their peasants would not pay taxes due to the monarchical state, since the landowners also wanted to avoid their own state taxes. When master artisans broke laws about the workplace that were meant to protect apprentices and control the output of commodities to prevent price-lowering over-supply, they were encouraged to do so by the new entrepreneurial merchants who wanted cheaper goods to trade for profit. Mainly, though, it was the middle class who encouraged popular illegality as a means of chipping away at the regal state's control of the marketplace: 'the bourgeoisie had needed these transformations; and economic growth was due, in part, to them. Tolerance then became encouragement' (84).

Yet by the second half of the eighteenth century, the bourgeoisie began to change its mind about popular illegality, mainly because they became more established and wealthier and began to realize that illegality would harm them more than the King. As France developed into a more commercial society in the passage from the first to the second half of the eighteenth century, the 'principal target of popular illegality tended to be not so much rights, as goods: pilfering and theft tended to replace smuggling and the armed struggle against the tax agents' (84). Additionally, as more of the middle class began to own farmland and wanted to move to 'intensive agriculture' to make the land more profitable, they resented the older 'tolerated practices' by peasants and small farmers that the local nobles had accepted (85). When 'landed property became absolute property' (85), something that could be bought and sold along with its products beyond the local region, the new owners regarded the old practices of 'free pasture, wood-collecting…quite simply as theft… [t]he illegality of rights, which often meant the survival of the most deprived, tended, with the new status of property, to become an illegality of property. It then had to be punished' (85).

Even more serious for the bourgeoisie than popular illegality in the countryside was its occurrence in the urban workplaces and port warehouses, where super-profitable commodities, like Caribbean sugar, were stored. Citing the work of London's eighteenth-century police commissioner Patrick Colquhoun, Foucault mentions the period's concern about pilfering and that a new urban network of illegality was emerging wherein the working class was complicit with organized crime. Managers might collude with workers, and workers would either allow gangs to steal from the warehouses, in return for a payoff, or would themselves pilfer goods and sell them to fences. Counterfeiting money was also a significant problem as it helped to debase and devalue currency, thus lowering the merchant's relative profit.

'With the new forms of capital accumulation, new relations of production and the new legal status of property' (86), the older forms of popular practices had to be more rigorously criminalized with the introduction of new laws and means of policing. The older 'economy of illegalities was restructured with the development of capitalist society' (87). Yet in doing so, the middle class made sure to create 'the first of the great loopholes in legality' (87) by separating the 'illegality of property' from the 'illegality of rights' (87). This distinction came from the difference wherein the illegality of theft was the one 'most accessible to the lower classes', while the bourgeoisie reserved for itself 'the illegality of rights', knowing that they could escape punishment for the latter by their greater familiarity with the law and ability to afford lawyers. Thus the middle class created for themselves 'the possibility of getting round its own regulations and its own laws' by creating two different kinds of courts (87). Today this is the distinction we make between criminal courts and ones that deal with 'civil' (white-collar) crime.

Foucault argues that penal reform, therefore, came out of a dual conflict: on one hand, against the 'super-power' of the monarch, who could not be brought before regular forms of justice and the infra-power of the working class in the midst of society. Over time, though, 'priority was given to the second' (89), as there was the push for a 'stricter and more constant control' (88) over the people by creating new forms of police and powers to punish. The penal system had to be changed to 'administer illegalities differentially, not to eliminate them all' (89). A separation had to be made between what the middle class could do against the (monarchy's) law and what the lower class was not allowed to do against the middle class.

The 'pressure' to change 'popular illegalities' became, from the time of the Revolution onward 'an essential imperative' for the middle class, and it was because of this need to protect property 'that reform was able to pass from the project state to that of an institution and set of practices' (89). Foucault seems to suggest that the writing of prison reformers was merely a 'project', an idea for change. These ideas became a 'set of practices' only when they were tied to 'institution[s]' as the middle class materialized the ideas of the moral reformers. But these humanitarian ideals were only implemented in a form best suited to the middle class's tactical interests.

The new model of punishment is now modelled on that which the middle class is most comfortable with handling: marketplace exchanges, where the contract is a document that ensures the exchange of money for goods and services. As Foucault notes, '[a]t the level of principles, this new strategy falls easily into the general theory of the contract' (89), rather than the notion of being dependent on the King's grace. Once the model of exchange was made the standard of behaviour, it became easier to criminalize the old form of tacit illegalities that were based on collective, oral customary assumptions rather than written, individualizing contractual relations.

In this way, the criminal is now seen as having broken their implied contract regarding universal standard behaviour. Instead of the criminal being an opponent to the prince, he or she is now an enemy of the 'entire social body' (90). 'The right to punish has been shifted from the vengeance of the sovereign to the defence of society' (90). Instead of the monarch having absolute authority as a 'super-power', an abstract or generalized 'society' now takes precedence.

This idea of society as one constructed through contracts rather than informal customs allows for the object and scale of punishment to be dedicated to the protection of property. It facilitated the advent of new tactics that could 'reach a target that is now more subtle but also more widely spread in the social body' (i.e. not the rare nobility, but the more common working class) (89). Foucault says that to police this numerically larger group, 'new principles for regularizing, refining, universalizing the art of punishing' (89) had to be developed so that the application of power could be made more homogenous (the generalized punishment of the section's title) in order to make it cheaper, politically more efficient and more prevalent in new social arenas. Foucault states unambiguously that the essential reason for penal reform was simultaneously to help 'constitute a new economy' (of capitalism) and a 'new technology of the power to punish' (the lower classes) (89).

It might seem that the middle-class desire to set up its model of social contracts is in conflict with humanitarian sensibility, but Foucault implies that this call of the heart was useful to the idea of contracts, since it, too, 'bears within it a principle of calculation' (91) that was used within a 'techno-politics of punishment' (92) of the new economy. Instead of the monarch who craves revenge, the middle class wants to punish as a means of avoiding future crimes. For the bourgeoisie a crime is not punished retroactively to destroy the act of crime, it is punished preemptively, as a deterrent to other, potential crimes. In this way, there comes a merger between those middle-class interests that want every individual to act as someone who rationally balances their desire to commit crime against the risk of punishment, as if they were calculating the costs and benefits of a trade, and the reformers who wanted to find a non-physical means of punishment.

Because society should look humane (and thus innocent of anger), punishment should not be violent. Yet the visual experience of punishment should cause some form of emotional response as a lesson to the audience. The audience was as key here as it had been in the prior phase of terror, but unlike the latter where the viewer was meant to be overwhelmed by the violence of the punishment, the audience member is asked to be 'rational' and calculate their own sympathetic, emotional response.

This fusion of feeling and calculation raised some questions though. Jurists worried about what to do with a spontaneous *'crime passionel'* (crime of passion) (100), since it is, by its very nature, illogical and occurs without the person thinking of the consequences. Consequently, it is not clear that punishing these crimes would help deter 'future disorder' (93). Additionally, there was the theoretical uncertainty about '[t]he last crime' (93). The point of punishment is to prevent others from repeating it, but if someone like Robinson Crusoe committed a crime alone on the island, then would it still be necessary to punish him? Does an act only become a crime if there is someone else who could potentially be affected by the punishment?

Despite these theoretical worries, punishment shifted from being enacted through the spectacular display of excessive force to a more calibrated mechanism where justice officials sought to 'punish exactly enough to prevent repetition' (93). The result was the rise of semiotic punishment, a system of codes and signs, where the body is used as a field of representation that can be seen (or read about) by others. This new 'semio-technique' (94) had to follow certain rules, just as did the prior mode of torture. Foucault lists six rules.

Punishment had to be only slightly greater than the act of the crime, so as to act as a deterrent, but in a way that the punishment seems rational and fair (the 'rule of minimum quantity'). Punishment had to focus on creating an *idea* of punishment in the audience, rather than the spectacle of physical pain (the 'rule of sufficient ideality' – ideal as in deriving from the imagination). Punishment was meant to make the criminal and the viewer feel averse to committing a future crime and was regarded as most preventive when it was specialized to fit the crime (the 'rule of lateral effects', a sidewise movement from criminal to audience) (94).

Punishment for a crime must be easily known and publicized. Laws must be written in a code that can be printed and circulated so that all can understand them outside of oral gossip, rumour and the uncertainty inherent in the irregularities of the regal courts (the 'rule of perfect certainty') (95). Punishment must be done in a way that follows the rule of common sense: 'the judge must use not ritual forms, but common instruments, that reason possessed by everyone' (97). The Inquisition's use of circumstantial evidence is to be replaced by a trial that is a forensic display of 'empirical research' where guilt is proven deductively, not inductively (97). The courtroom must be like a laboratory searching for a scientific proof that is no longer dependent on a confession (the 'rule of common truth'). Lastly, the legal code should be so precise as to prevent the confusions and ambiguities of the monarchical codes. The legal code should be totalizing enough so that it could not 'harbour the hope of impunity' (98). Punishment must fit the crime, especially since punishment is mimetic and must re-enact the crime for all to see (the 'rule of optimal specification').

These rules created the pressure for two different, but inter-linked results. On the one hand, there needed to be a complete table of categories in which all crimes could be placed, but, on the other, there was the 'need for an individualization of sentences, in accordance with the particular characteristics of each criminal' (99).

This individualization would lead, later in the nineteenth century, to a system where a 'psychological knowledge' (99) of the criminal's personality, desires and motives would be even more important than the system by which the presence of guilt was proven. But the 'code-individualization' (99) link is not yet a dominant feature at this historical point in the eighteenth century. Instead, the concern for 'anthropological individualization' (100) was still being driven by the period's leading interest in forming natural history-like classifications, wherein a taxonomy of crimes is akin to the taxonomy of creatures. The creation of these categories was felt to be urgent, even though it was not yet entirely clear how 'to apply fixed laws to particular individuals' (100).

The main challenge for this phase, therefore, was how to establish a politically motivated redefinition of illegality and a way of making punishment both general and specific to crimes. As a result, two different 'lines of objectification of crime and the criminal' (101) were proposed. One presents the criminal as so alienated from society that he or she stands as an 'abnormal' monster, a 'wild fragment of nature' (101). The other argues for a 'scientific' approach that will measure the effects of punishment in relation to the crime in the way of 'treatment' to prevent the recurrence of crime. Historically, the first approach took longer to develop. For the second, the writers of the late Enlightenment (the *Idéologues*, or early writers about the power of ideas) devoted themselves to developing a 'theory of interests, representations and signs' as a 'sort of general recipe for the exercise of power over men: the "mind" as a surface of inscription for power, with semiology as its tool; the submission of bodies through the control of ideas; the analysis of representations as a principle in a politics of bodies that was much more effective than the ritual anatomy of torture and execution' (102). Foucault here once more juxtaposes this

How to Read Foucault's *Discipline and Punish*

new 'technology of subtle, effective, economic powers' with 'the sumptuous expenditure of the power of the sovereign' (102). To drive home his point, he cites from a 1767 text by the French jurist and philosopher J.M. Servan to illustrate how the Enlightenment ideals of reason substituted a belief in absolutist rule in penal discourse:

> A stupid despot may constrain his slaves with iron chains; but a true politician binds them even more strongly by the chain of their own ideas; it is at the stable point of reason that he secures the end of the chain; this link is all the stronger in that we do not know of what it is made and we believe it to be our own work; despair and time eat away the bonds of iron and steel, but they are powerless against the habitual union of ideas, they can only tighten it still more; and on the soft fibres of the brain is founded the unshakable base of the soundest of Empires. (102–3)

Foucault ends this section, though, by indicating that semio-techniques and ideas will quickly lead to a 'new politics of the body' (103). However, unlike the torture/terror system, which works on the body's outside, the new punishment system works on the interior mind, the 'soft fibres of the brain', and will be associated with a different kind of (class) rule. In the next section, Foucault describes the mechanism for this mental surgery.

2. The gentle way in punishment

Foucault continues his description of the late eighteenth century's renovation of punishment as a 'technology of representation' (104) and he lists six characteristics of this new kind of punishment.

Firstly, punishment must be seen to be natural and unarbitrary. The period's reformers desired that there should be as close a link as possible between the punishment and the crime, one mirroring the other, so that it seems like the punishment is not an irrational expression of (the monarch's) caprice, but a logical, calm and natural consequence of crime. In the words of one reformer, '"then penalties no longer proceed from the will of the legislator, but from the nature of things"' (105). This form of punishment differs from torture because it is no longer 'violence'. There should be a 'reasonable aesthetic of punishment' (106), with a 'transparency of the sign to that which it signifies... a relation that is immediately intelligible to the senses' (106). The period's justice consequently tries to rationally match the punishment closely to the crime: fines for thieves, poison for poisoners, murder by the death penalty and so on. If torture depended on the crude display of the sovereign's power in the body of the condemned, the new punishment is characterized by a subtler mode of control: 'power must act while concealing itself' (106).

Secondly, the sign of punishment must not only equal the crime, it should strike at *the desire* to commit crime. The purpose of punishment should be to regenerate the intrinsic virtue believed to exist in all individuals, which has only been weakened in ways that led to a crime being committed. Punishment is still a play of forces, not in the retributive sense of the older monarchical mode, but in a fashion that seeks to restore the individual to their natural good behaviour. Punishment is supposed to repair the damaged perpetrator of crime.

Thirdly, if punishment is dedicated to the transformation of the individual, then it must have an aspect of change within it as well. There needs to be an element of 'temporal modulation' (107) in the sentence. Except for 'incorrigibles' (107), punishment must not last forever, since a permanent punishment would remove the idea that the criminal can be recuperated. Punishments, therefore, need to have different durations and intensities of punishment according to the crime.

Fourthly, because punishment is supposed to teach a lesson, the viewing public is as much a target in the act of punishing as the guilty individual. Unlike the scaffold, the point is not to create terror and fear in the viewers, but to educate and convince them that punishment is reasonable, firstly, because the criminal has attacked 'society' and secondly, that the force of punishment is rational in its effort to protect everyone, since we are all equally damaged by crime's dissolving of the social contract that governs all behaviour. 'In the old system, the body of the condemned man became the King's property, on which the sovereign left his mark… [n]ow [the condemned man] will be rather the property of society, the object of a collective and useful appropriation' (109). Punishment must be visible, for all to see, because when the criminal is seen as working for public good, such as on a chain-gang fixing roads, the 'collective interest in the punishment of the condemned man' is achieved (109). A 'crime-punishment sign' (109) is reinforced throughout the general community.

Fifthly, to achieve the goal of public education and consent to punishment, a new 'learned economy of publicity' (109) is created through the dissemination of printed signs and public displays of paraded criminals that mourn the criminal's departure from society because of her or his crime. In the prior monarchical system

> the example was based on terror: physical fear, collective horror, images that must be engraved on the memories of the spectators, like the brand on the cheek or shoulder of the condemned man. The example is now based on the lesson, the discourse, the decipherable sign, the representation of public morality. (110)

Instead of the 'ambiguous festivals of the Ancien Régime' (110), public punishment in the Enlightenment period should make it difficult for the citizen to ignore the law or recognize that crime separates you from society. Therefore, each element of the public punishment must be legible and repeated as much as possible as a public lesson. '[P]unishments must be a school rather than a festival; an ever-open book rather than a ceremony' (111). For this reason, any punishment conducted in secrecy wastes the chance for public education. In this light, prison reformers thought that crime should literally be a learning moment and schoolchildren should be taken to places of punishment as part of their civic education into how a citizen should or should not act.

Sixthly, the criminal must not seem glorious or heroic in these representations, which should 'arrest the desire to commit' crime (112). In this light, the reformers wanted these enactments to be constantly dispersed throughout society, wherever crime could occur. 'Gentle' punishment turns the criminal's body into a book that educates throughout 'the punitive city' full of 'tiny theatres of punishment' (113) where 'in counterpoint with all the direct examples of virtue, one may at each moment encounter, as a living spectacle, the misfortunes of vice' (113). The signs educating the public about the consequences of crime consist of 'placards, different-coloured caps bearing inscriptions, posters, symbols, texts read or printed, [that] tirelessly repeat the code' (113). The frequent experience and persistence of punishment in the everyday makes its lessons enter the collective unconscious. The carnival-like 'ritual of the public execution' is thus replaced by 'this serious theatre, with its multifarious and persuasive scenes' (113).

Starting a new section, Foucault now begins to set up a conceptual problem that he tries to resolve in the remainder of this segment and in Part Three: of all the methods of punishment, one was never considered 'in these projects for specific, visible and "telling" penalties': imprisonment (114). Yet, 'within a short space of time, detention became the essential form of punishment' (115). Imprisonment was initially considered unsuitable as a punishment because it lacked any specificity to the crimes; was useless for public education because the criminal was hidden from view; was expensive to maintain; trained people in criminal pursuits through prolonged contact with other criminals; and exposed prisoners to the despotism of the guards, the modern replacement of the all-powerful King. Against the theory for visible representation, prison was 'obscurity, violence and suspicion' (115). If the point of punishment was to transport penality's representations through the city, the hidden, enclosed space of prison was unacceptable.

How is it, then, Foucault asks, that in the nineteenth century, prison had unexpectedly, and paradoxically, become the 'essential form of punishment' (115) and plans were made to build multiple prisons throughout the nation? Foucault summarizes as follows:

> The scaffold, where the body of the criminal had been exposed to the ritually manifested force of the sovereign, the punitive theatre in which the representation of punishment was permanently available to the social body, was replaced by a great enclosed, complex and hierarchized structure that was integrated into the very body of the state apparatus. A quite different materiality, a quite different physics of power, a quite different way of investing men's bodies had emerged. (115–16)

So in less than twenty years, the principles of the revolutionary 1790s had vanished, 'almost instantaneously' (116), making imprisonment the standard punishment for nearly all crimes both in France and throughout Europe. To achieve this turn, several prejudices against prison had to be overcome. Imprisonment was previously something that was either only a temporary measure device, where people were detained only until their real punishment could occur, or as substitute for those who could not physically handle other kinds of punishment, such as women, children and invalids (118). Additionally, prison was associated in the public's mind with 'arbitrary royal decision' (119) where people could be imprisoned on the whim of those in power. The French national holiday celebrates the start of the Revolution with the date of the public destruction of a prison, the Bastille. For the reformers, detention was a 'privileged instrument of despotism' (119) and thus unacceptable to a rational society. So the return to imprisonment could only occur if the public was given an alternative explanation for how prisons would function in a postmonarchical society.

Foucault suggests that the explanation usually given for the unexpected return and rise of the modern prison is that prestigious, new models of punitive improvement came from outside France, each with their own renovation of the purpose and procedures of imprisonment. The first model was that of the Rasphuis, created in 1596 in Amsterdam. This prison allowed for discretion by prison administrators (rather than judges) to shorten the time in prison based on good conduct; create mandatory waged work for prisoners; install a strict time-table of daily activities; and establish a system of rewards and moral encouragement. A prison in Ghent also emphasized the need for work as a means of teaching virtue to prisoners and of offsetting the operating costs of the prison. Work became a required therapy for the criminal's moral reconstruction and a means of training the corrupt individual into a more correct worker, a 'homo oeconomicus' (122). This turn forms 'the link between the theory, so characteristic of the sixteenth century, of a pedagogical and spiritual transformation of individuals brought about by continuous exercise, and the penitentiary techniques conceived in the second half of the eighteenth century' (121).

Penal labour, especially for those captured for begging or vagabondage, also had 'economic imperatives' (121), as it helped pay for criminal prosecutions and lost tax money that was spent to compensate property owners for damages caused by vagabonds; it lowered costs for bosses by forcing non-prison labourers to accept lower wages, because they had to compete against prison labour, and it reduced the government's welfare costs, since only the 'true poor' (121) would receive state charity.

The next model of the 'reformatory' (123) came in the late eighteenth century as English prisons added the concept of isolation as an essential part of correction. Because the prison 'community' of criminals provides bad examples, prisoners need to be isolated in cells as a therapeutic space for self-reflection to improve 'the moral subject' alongside training '*homo oeconomicus*' (123). This sequestration shifts punishment from the sociability of the prior system, where prisoners spent time bundled together during their labour in public work projects or parades. Instead of the prisoner being shown publicly in a group, the jailed were cut off from human contact, even with each other.

Finally, and most importantly, came the Philadelphia model, 'no doubt the most famous because it was associated' (123) with American democracy and did not fail as quickly as had so many other new kinds of model prisons. The chief example here is Philadelphia's Walnut Street Prison (1790) organized by Quakers. It combined features of the Ghent and Gloucester systems in that there was mandatory work, a time-table of work, eating and sleeping schedules, aspects of solitary confinement and the ability to shorten the sentence if good behaviour was demonstrated.

Walnut Street, however, added three significant aspects to the mix: firstly, prisoners were not to be routinely observed by the public; secondly, prison was an enclosed space for a prisoner to be transformed by the administration; finally, and most importantly, prison was a site for the 'development of a knowledge of the individuals' (125). When a prisoner entered, the prison administrators had a complete dossier about the prisoner's crime, its circumstances, police examination and comments on the person's behaviour. This case file would serve as the basis for the administrators to organize prisoners 'not so much according to their crimes as according to the dispositions that they revealed. The prison became a sort of permanent observatory that made it possible to distribute the varieties of vice or weakness' (126). A 'whole corpus of individualizing knowledge' focused on 'not so much the crime committed...but the potentiality of danger that lies hidden in an individual and which is manifested in his observed everyday conduct' (126). As a 'permanent observatory', the prison became an 'apparatus of knowledge [*savoir*]' (126).

There were similarities and differences between the ideas of the eighteenth-century reformers and the new discourse of the reformatories. Both sought not to 'efface a crime, but to prevent its repetition' (126). They meant to transform the criminal's future, not blot out his past actions. Similarly, both sought to reform the criminal through individualized punishment.

But here the similarity ends. The 'difference is to be found in the procedure of access to the individual, the way in which the punishing power gets control over him, the instruments that it uses in order to achieve this transformation' (127), as well as 'the technology of the penalty, not in its theoretical foundations; in the relation that it establishes with the body and with the soul, and not in the way that it is inserted within the legal system' (127).

The prison reformers wanted to know what signs and representations would work to 'gain control of the individual' (127) and use it as a sign system to, in turn, control the public. The modern 'apparatus of corrective penality' (128) acts very differently. 'The point of application of the penalty is not the representation, but the body, time, everyday gestures and activities; ... [t]he body and the soul, as principles of behaviours, form the element that is now proposed for punitive intervention' (128). The 'studied manipulation of the individual', rather than 'an art of representations' (128), is the focus.

The instruments used are no longer the 'complexes of representation, reinforced and circulated' in the punishment scheme, but 'forms of coercion, schemata of constraint, applied and repeated' (128). Instead of signs, there should be exercises involving 'time-tables, compulsory movements, regular activities, solitary meditation, work in common, silence, application, respect, good habits' (128). Instead of the goal being to recreate a subject able to follow the 'social pact', as was the case in the prior mode, now there is the desire to create the 'obedient subject', one who is 'subjected to habits, rules, orders, an authority that is exercised continually around him and upon him, and which he must allow to function automatically in him' (128–9). The chief goals here are 'secrecy' and 'autonomy' for the prison, not the desire to get the public to see and oversee punishment. The 'punitive city' of the Enlightenment's public procession of signs is replaced by the 'coercive institution' (129) that is secretive and cut off from society. The rise of the prison system thus marks 'the institutionalization of the power to punish, or, to be more precise: [the] will [to] the power to punish' (130) as a means of gaining and then deploying information about the prisoner's psychology.

By the end of the eighteenth century, then, there were 'three ways of organizing the power to punish' (130). The first was the one involving the old monarchical law that saw punishment as a 'ceremonial of sovereignty' involving 'the ritual marks of the vengeance that it applies to the body of the condemned man', which publicly displayed 'the physical presence of the sovereign and of his power' and used 'before the eyes of the spectator an effect of terror' (130).

The second and third systems 'both refer to a preventive, utilitarian, corrective conception of the right to punish that belongs to society as a whole' (130). In the second, 'reforming jurists...saw punishment as a procedure for requalifying individuals as subjects' and they avoided marks on the body in favour of 'signs, coded sets of representations, which would be given the most rapid circulation and the most general acceptance possible by citizens witnessing the scene of punishment' (130–1). The third model of the prison institution envisaged punishment as a 'technique for the coercion of individuals' and 'operated methods of training the body...in the form of habits, in behaviour' run by administrators (131).

In the last pages of this section, Foucault presents for the first time descriptions of his tripartite historical scheme of power, which can be plotted out in tabular form (see Table 2.1). Foucault argues that these technologies cannot simply be understood as effects of different theories of law or as coming from specific institutions, or moral attitudes. They are all forms that emerge as strategies. The question, though, remains, why from these three models of regal terror, enlightenment/revolutionary representation and discipline, the third one was 'adopted' for the modern period. This is the riddle that Foucault answers in the following, third part.

Table 2.1

Period	Form of Penality	Dominant Power	Criminal as	Process	Object	Site	Result
Ancien Régime	Terror/ Torture	Sovereign/ Absolute Monarch	Vanquished enemy	Ceremony of vengeance	Tortured body	Scaffold	Mark (scar)
Late 18C	Punishment	(Enlight-enment) Society	Semiotic subject	Circulation of representation	Soul with representa-tions	City streets	Sign
19C on-ward	Discipline	Bourgeois institutions	Reformable subject	Exercise of the body	Body subject to training	Institu-tion	Trace (soul)

Part Three: Discipline

The third part is the one that is most commonly assigned to students and that occasional or second-hand readers of *Discipline and Punish* are familiar with. It is the source for many of Foucault's most quoted terms and phrases. While it is the chapter that you may find yourself returning to re-read often, it is advisable to do so only with careful attention to the Parts before and after it. Part Four is especially important, since it is there that Foucault explains the purpose of most of the techniques he describes in Part Three.

1. Docile bodies

Foucault begins this section by describing the definition and evolution of the modern, disciplined body within an increasingly quasi-militaristic society. He starts by contrasting two ideals of the soldier in different historical periods. In the early seventeenth century, under the *Ancien Régime*, an excellent soldier was one who could display his superior, martial physique as an immobile object. By the 'classical age', the name Foucault uses for the eighteenth-century period of the Enlightenment (classical in its rediscovery of 'Greek' and 'Roman' history and culture, when the middle classes began to recirculate tales about the Roman Republic as examples of alternative legal and political structures to the absolutist monarchy), the individual body was discovered as 'object and target of power' (136), a body that can be made more skilful and effective. This technically mutable body was considered more important than one of unprefabricated 'natural' strength and good 'blood'. Just as the early phase of the Industrial Revolution was discovering new production processes and technologies, there was a complementary notion that the human individual (and society) could be reconstructed to be better and more efficient. The heroic ideal of untouched nature became replaced with one of technical betterment.

Returning to the example of de La Mettrie's *Man-the-Machine* [L'Homme-machine], Foucault argues that the discovery of the body as an object that can be 'manipulated, shaped, trained, [and] which obeys, responds, becomes skilful and increases its forces' (136) – a manufactured body – works through two registers: the 'anatomico-metaphysical register', which seeks to detail the body's functions, and the 'technico-political register', which uses calculations and quantifications, mainly gathered from armies, schools and hospitals, to make bodies submissive and controllable. These two registers of the body as object of study – 'analysable body' on the one hand and the 'manipulable body' on the other hand – combine to form the project of 'docility'. 'A body is docile that may be subjected, used, transformed and improved' (136). This is a two-stage process. The body must first be made submissive and docile before it can be 'subjected, used, transformed and improved'.

Foucault argues that these 'projects of docility' were new in the scale, object and mode of their control. Firstly, instead of trying to make large groups, or populations, submissive, as a conquering nation might with a colonized one, 'docility' works on the smaller scale of individuals. Secondly, the object of concern is not the body's messages or representations, but its forces and dynamics. The body is not meant to 'signify', as it was in the age of punishment, but to be 'economic'; it must be made efficient and trained through exercise. Finally, 'docility' creates a mode of total supervision, where the individual faces an 'uninterrupted, constant coercion' through the new use of 'time, space, movement', which are segmented into smaller units, and 'the processes of the activity' are even more important than 'its result' (137).

These three methods (focus on the individual; make it productive; supervise its duration, location and trajectory) combine to form what Foucault calls 'discipline'. The term 'discipline' implies both the controlling or disciplining of a person and a 'discipline' as an academic specialty (a knowledge of each body, of bodies, will be produced). 'Discipline' is the name that Foucault gives to the combination of the practical and theoretical attempts to make the body both docile and more useful (increase its utility).

docility + utility = discipline

While *aspects* of these disciplinary methods have already long existed, they cross a threshold as they converge in a new and distinctive way 'in the course of the seventeenth and eighteenth centuries' when 'the disciplines became general formulas of domination' (137). Modern discipline is different from older models in the ways it controls bodies. Discipline is not like the traditional form of slavery because the latter takes violent command of the whole body: discipline works more subtly, it does not appropriate the entire body (as would torture) and consequently does not require as much muscular force as a slave-owner must dispense. Discipline differs from a servant's relationship to the master, since, as we will see, discipline does not have a central, king-like, voice of authority; discipline is more decentralized, diffuse and universal. Discipline differs from feudal serfdom because it does not seek the spectacular 'ritual marks of allegiance' (137) to the lord. Finally, discipline cannot be compared to monastic asceticism, which seeks to 'obtain renunciations rather than increases of utility' (137); the monastery wants the individual to give up his or her body and abstain from its use, while discipline wants individuals to make their bodies more useful.

Discipline seeks a new 'art of the human body' (137) that creates a relationship where obedience and productivity are mutually constituting. 'Discipline increases the forces of the body (in economic terms of utility) and diminishes these same forces (in political terms of obedience)' (138). The body is not only made to do more, but the process of gaining useful labour is made easier to control as well.

From here, Foucault increasingly telegraphs his argument that there is a fundamental relationship between capitalism and discipline as he insists that discipline is a key, albeit previously under-recognized, aspect of the rise of capitalism. 'Disciplinary coercion' is what enables the 'economic exploitation [that] separates the force and the product of labour' (138) from the proletarian for the capitalist's profit. For Marx, profit comes from altering the mode of production to produce a new surplus-value through the exploitation of labourers. For Foucault, discipline is the social and political mechanism that facilitates the economic control on which a bourgeois society rests, since discipline provides the techniques for controlling labourers (docility) in ways that increase their profit-making productivity (utility). An older form of marxist criticism would see the political as simply mirroring the economic. Foucault suggests that the two are inextricably intertwined and mutually affirming, rather than one being dependent on the other. 'If economic exploitation separates the force and the product of labour, let us say that disciplinary coercion establishes in the body the constricting link between an increased aptitude and an increased domination' (138). Rather than substituting marxist analysis, Foucault arguably builds on and refines it to illustrate exactly how capitalism holds individuals in its grip.

Discipline is not a centralized system of control; it is diffuse and discrete:

> The 'invention' of this new political anatomy must not be seen as a sudden discovery. It is rather a multiplicity of often minor processes, of different origin and scattered location, which overlap, repeat, or imitate one another, support one another, distinguish themselves from one another according to their domain of application, converge and gradually produce the blueprint of a general method. (138)

These aspects are first seen in secondary education, then primary education, then hospitals and finally the military. The tempo of circulation in aspects of discipline between these different institutional sites is always different, sometimes fast, sometimes slow. But '[o]n almost every occasion they were adopted in response to particular needs:

an industrial innovation, a renewed outbreak of certain epidemic diseases, the invention of the rifle or the victories of Prussia' (138).

The key implication in this claim that modern power works through a decentralized network is that Foucault suggests that there is not just one force, like the State, that can be overthrown to liberate people. Instead, we are held in place by a capillary network of multiple small nodes, each of which contributes to our subordination, but which can also be compensated for if one fails or is dismantled. The battlegrounds for Foucault are more numerous than traditional political science has considered.

Commenting on his method and the scope of this study, Foucault says that he does not intend to write 'the history of the different disciplinary institutions'; instead, he wishes 'to map on a series of examples some of the essential techniques that most easily spread from one to another' (139). His examples, he reveals in a footnote on page 141, are drawn from 'military, medical, educational and industrial institutions' (314). As Foucault notes, '[o]ther examples might have been taken from colonization, slavery and child rearing' (314). This note and its implications have caused a fair amount of debate, since it can be read as suggesting that the histories of the empire and gender are simply redundant and that race and gender do not have specific aspects that need treating. While this may not be what Foucault meant to say, this rather cursory footnote is admittedly less than helpful.

Rather than writing minute descriptions of different institutional histories, then, Foucault concentrates on what he believes is a general tendency within each of them: a 'new micro-physics' (139) of control that spreads throughout society in small, often unnoticed ways. He will mainly focus on the prison as his representative model (for the others).

Returning to analyse the distinctive qualities of discipline, Foucault insists that discipline is an unusual form of power that is often difficult to discern. The agents of discipline are preoccupied with minor, seemingly inconsequential things because they realize that power can be managed more efficiently and with less resistance through rules over small things. 'Discipline is a political anatomy of detail' (139). Foucault acknowledges that aspects of the 'utilitarian rationalization of detail in moral accountability and political control' (139) have existed historically before in 'theology and asceticism' (140), but he thinks that what is new here is the secular importance given to making details productive. The figure that he chooses to characterize this is the new State figure of control, Napoleon Bonaparte. Foucault invokes Napoleon here because the General represents the militarizing of French society through the rise of the Empire: 'Napoleon did not discover this world; but we know that he set out to organize it; and he wished to arrange around him a mechanism of power that would enable him to see the smallest event that occurred in the state he governed' (141).

Before moving on to Foucault's summary of discipline, it is also worth pausing to recognize that Foucault often refers back to Church theology to show the initial appearance, but not functional lineage, of modern discipline. He does this partly because France is, of course, a Catholic dominated country, and so any historian of France is going to end up looking at Church archives. But this gesture also counters a familiar argument in historical sociology, one most clearly made by Max Weber (1864–1920) in *The*

Protestant Ethic and the Spirit of Capitalism, which sees Protestantism as providing the key aspect to the rise of capitalism. *Discipline and Punish* can be read as rejecting this narrowly denominational explanation. To downplay the importance of Protestantism, Foucault uses many examples from Catholic writers and institutions to show alternative pathways. The larger point is that Foucault sees the origin of discipline as emerging from the rise of secular institutions and does not see religious cultures as being the leading force for changes.

Foucault now describes the four different aspects of discipline involving the control, classification and regulation of space, time, human development and its dynamics. The first is *the art of distributions* involving the organization and fixing of 'individuals in space' (141). There are several techniques herein. Firstly, individuals must be *enclosed*, contained within nonpermeable spaces, like barracks, schools and factories. These spaces will literally be walled in to prevent or supervise the movement of individuals in and out of defined areas. The model is the monastic cell, separated from public view. The aim is to control space to prevent rebellion, to hold the vagabond mass in place, to master the placement of the labour force and fix it to desirable places.

Secondly, these closed-off spaces will be *partitioned* in smaller and smaller units. The purpose of making a divided, exclusive space is to prevent those who should be ruled from gathering in groups whose movement cannot be ascertained or controlled. It was a 'tactic of anti-desertion, anti-vagabondage, anti-concentration' (143). The traffic and gatherings of the lower classes are to be broken up and people placed in ways that make it easy to know where they are and what they are doing at any time. Partitioning makes for an 'analytical space' that allows for better supervision than poorly defined spaces of social exchanges, like ports. In no case should the lower classes be allowed to have meeting-places where they might dangerously circulate political ideas and stolen or pilfered goods.

Thirdly, spaces are also to be '*functional sites*' (143) that not only allow people to be more easily supervised individually, but also to make them become more economically 'useful' (144) in these spaces. Space is considered as 'therapeutic' in the sense of positioning individuals in ways that they can function 'better', that is to say more efficiently than before (144). The model here is the industrial division of labour where one part of the factory is responsible for only one aspect of a commodity's production. The liberal economist Adam Smith (1723–1790) celebrated this division of labour as increasing workers' efficiency and Marx saw it as a defining aspect of the capitalist transformation in the late eighteenth/nineteenth century. Foucault similarly sees the 'emergence of large-scale industry' as dependent on the 'division of the production process, the individual-izing fragmentation of labour power' (145) through spatial divisions. Functional space is made legible by charting it out on a two-dimensional table or grid graph.

Finally, space must have a *rank* (145); it must be divided into interchangeable units, and ones that are always organized in a hierarchical sequence. An individual's value is determined by where they are located within 'serial space' (147) as a means of encouraging them to do more. Foucault's example here is the classroom that is divided into seats where supposedly smarter or more worthy students are placed in relation to others who perform less well.

Foucault illustrates this point with the example of a Jesuit school that uses classical Roman names to describe its competition-inducing ranks, and he says that '[o]ne should not forget, that generally speaking, the Roman model, at the Enlightenment, played a dual role: in its republican aspect, it was the embodiment of liberty; in its military aspect, it was the ideal schema of discipline' (146). This phrase goes to the heart of Foucault's critique about the contradictions inherent in the anti-aristocratic, republican Enlightenment. The middle classes that promoted the Enlightenment and the French Revolution sought to legitimize themselves by way of historical examples from the Roman Republic, but Foucault reminds us that this was a republic that also became a military empire. Once more, Foucault wants to show that 'reason' (knowledge) is always tied to 'force' (power).

Foucault suggests that this two-fold model made for the inevitability of Napoleon as Emperor coming out of the French Revolution. Aside from criticizing the latent force within bourgeois slogans of equality, Foucault also seems to be making a coded comment about the repressiveness of Stalin as emerging from the Russian Revolution, in other words, the failure of the Russian Revolution to question bourgeois justice and other kinds of institutions alongside the overthrowing of a capitalist economy. This implicit critique works to reflect back on the French Communist Party (PCF) which was/is very Stalinist and was blamed for not supporting the student movement in 'May 1968'. In a larger sense, Foucault seems to telegraph his interest in looking back at why the recent social movements of the 1960s were not able to succeed, and he does this by looking at the history of other failed revolutions, like that of the 1790s.

Summarizing the division of space, Foucault says that, 'the disciplines create complex spaces that are at once architectural, functional and hierarchical' (148). Distribution makes:

cells	architectural space	fixes positions and prevents circulation
places	functional space	marks places with an indicative value
ranks	hierarchical space	makes individuals obedient

The method that brought all these together was the use of a table. 'The drawing up of "tables" was one of the great problems of the scientific, political and economic technology of the eighteenth century' (148). '[T]he table was both a technique of power and a procedure of knowledge' (148) as it allowed authorities to organize large groups by providing an instrument that provided an 'order' that could allow it to be controlled and mastered to gain productivity, a 'cellular power' (149) or power that comes from the creation of spaces in cells. The power of the table comes from how the 'twin operations in which the two elements – distribution and analysis, supervision and intelligibility – are inextricably bound up' (148). Importantly, this strategy of the table facilitates the controlling of both individuals and groups of people: 'disciplinary tactics is situated on the axis that links the singular and the multiple. It allows both the characterization of the individual as individual and the ordering of a given multiplicity' (149).

After the division of space, the second aspect of discipline involves time and the 'control of activity' (149). Just as with space, Foucault details a similar number of features of the disciplinary redeployment of time, many of which echo Marx's comments in *Capital*.

The chief of these is the *time-table*, the numerical organization of time, similar to how the geometric table organizes space. Time is not simply detailed for how it should be spent, but it is turned into sequenced activities that are constantly supervised to constitute 'a totally useful time' (150) through the removal of distractions. This rationalization creates a time-work discipline that is often called Taylorization after the mechanical engineer and consultant Frederick Winslow Taylor (1856–1915) who studied work flows in factories with the goal of segmenting them into smaller, more efficient, steps to create greater divisions of labour. Foucault again traces the use of time to 'the religious orders' but notes that 'the disciplines altered these methods of temporal regulation from which they derived...by refining them. One began to count in quarter hours, in minutes, in seconds' (150).

Utility is thus created by the *temporal elaboration of the act* (151), which gives a timed value to physical acts. As '[t]ime penetrates the body and with it all the meticulous controls of power' (152), there will be a set programme – an 'anatomo-chronological schema of behaviour' (152) – that dictates how long everything should take, not more, not less.

Thirdly, there is the *correlation of the body and the gesture* (152) where the body is taught to act in certain, precise ways. We are trained in a 'gymnastics' of how we should hold our bodies and compose our physical gestures in order to achieve the efficiencies and time-keeping demanded by the prior two aspects of time discipline.

Fourthly, this disciplining means to have humans interact with objects through a new *body-object articulation* (153), where people become integrated with, rather than controllers of, non-animate processes. Foucault's examples are taken from the military, in particular the soldier's use of the rifle, but the driving force in this movement comes from the 'coercive link with the apparatus of production' (153), by which Foucault means the methods that ensure that workers assimilate to the rhythms of machinery, rather than the reverse. The body will be like a machine. Borrowing from military theoreticians, Foucault calls this training of the body a 'manoeuvre' (153). The body is not just exploited, it is also coercively taught to submit to a machinified 'apparatus of production'. Disciplinary power joins the human body and objects in a new relationship: 'Over the whole surface of contact between the body and the object it handles, power is introduced, fastening them to one another. It constitutes a body-weapon, body-tool, body-machine complex' (153).

The final aspect of time is '*exhaustive use*', the 'principle of non-idleness' or wasting time that 'was counted by God and paid for by men' (154). Time-wasting was a 'moral offence and economic dishonesty' (154), the latter because employers who pay an hourly wage see any time that the labourer is not using to make commodities as 'stealing' time that could be used to generate wealth for the employer.

After these divisions of time and space, Foucault highlights the third aspect of discipline – human development. He somewhat awkwardly calls this process of development '*the organization of geneses*' (156), by which he means that the individual is placed in a pathway of personal development that will make her or him more useful, controllable and productive. This is the ideology of progressive evolution (genesis), where human nature is made to be productive on a schedule.

The organization of personal development, a 'time of individuals' (157), is achieved in four ways. Firstly, time is divided into successive segments that must end at a certain time. Secondly, these segments are put into an analytical plan or sequence where one follows the other in increasing difficulty or complexity. Thirdly, each segment must end with an examination that will allow the supervisors to differentiate, rank and classify every individual. Lastly, after this ranking each individual will be given a role and range of exercises suited to their position in the hierarchy.

The clearest example of this process, and the most immediately recognizable one for many readers of this book, is the practice of an 'analytical pedagogy' (159) in schools. Its processes of creating developmental times and spaces insist on judging our development through 'linear', 'evolutive' (160) time, where we pass from class to class and year to year:

> The 'seriation' of successive activities makes possible a whole investment of duration by power: the possibility of a detailed control and a regular intervention (of differentiation, correction, punishment, elimination) in each moment of time. ... Temporal dispersal is brought together to produce a profit, thus mastering a duration that would otherwise elude one's grasp. Power is articulated directly onto time; it assures its control and guarantees its use. (160)

We might also think of the pressure that making a résumé forces on us, where we have to make sure that all of our lifetime can be accounted for in productive ways that justify the next stage of our development or promotion. A bad résumé is one that has unexplained gaps.

Foucault suggests that these procedures also merged with a larger scale of control, for the 'two great "discoveries" of the eighteenth century – the progress of societies and the geneses of individuals – were perhaps correlative with the new techniques of power' (160). A new kind of history is now possible, not one of 'solemn events' but of 'continuous evolutions' (161), a history of cultural development. Foucault correlates each of these moments with different 'techniques of subjection': 'the "dynamics" of continuous evolutions tends to replace the "dynastics" of solemn events' (161). Although Foucault does not mention this implication explicitly, the civilizational ideal of development that came about in such a way was used for arguments where non-European societies could be presented as 'behind' European ones, but trainable to be like the more 'advanced' or 'developed' ones. This claim also laid the roots for social Darwinism, especially eugenics and theories of racial degeneration, since it was now possible to produce distinctions that saw people as more or less advanced along progressive history. Foucault calls the procedures at the centre of the individual's linear development '*exercise*', but it is a training that is never allowed to come to an end: 'Exercise, having become an element in the political technology of the body and of duration, does not culminate in a beyond, but tends towards a subjection that has never reached its limit' (162).

The fourth and last aspect of discipline involves the '*composition of forces*' (162), where all the separate parts or segments are fitted together in an efficient and productive complex. Citing directly from Marx's *Capital*, Foucault draws this comparison between military techniques and the problem of capitalist work relations where 'cooperation' (163) between large groups of workers in linked units makes the labour force of a mass of workers greater than the individual sum of their parts. The model here is the machine, which Marx defines as an articulated system of instruments. In the same way, a social machine has to be created by a 'carefully measured combination of forces' that is organized by a 'precise system of command' (166), which ideally is directed by clear and simple signs. Foucault here clearly builds on Marx to construct his own theory of 'discipline': 'Discipline is no longer simply an art of distributing bodies, of extracting time from them and accumulating it, but of composing forces in order to obtain an efficient machine' (164). There are three aspects of this composition. Firstly, the individual body is made to be a segment in a social machine. Secondly, time itself is also made to function like a machine. Lastly, the articulated system 'requires a precise system of command' involving 'signals' to help with the 'training' or *dressage* of bodies (166).

Now Foucault reviews his argument, which can also be put in tabular form (Table 3.1). This table of disciplinary techniques can also be written as in Table 3.2. For Foucault, these 'tactics' form the general strategy of militarizing society (167). The eighteenth century 'saw the birth of the great political and military strategy by which nations confronted each other's economic and demographic forces; but it also saw the birth of meticulous military and political tactics by which the control of bodies and individual forces was exercised within states' (168). While we traditionally think of the Enlightenment period as focused on rationality

Table 3.1

Discipline creates:

4 types of individuality through
cellular (spatial distribution)
organic (codes activities)
genetic (accumulates time)
combinatory (composition of forces)

4 techniques
drawing up tables (groups are contained and watched)
prescribing movements (proper manoeuvres indicate standards)
imposing exercises (exercise is tied to an idea of progress)
arranging tactics (forges new collective identities)

Table 3.2

Activity	Object	Techniques	Instruments	Method
Art of distribution	Space (architecture)	Cellular	Grid Plane (cells, places, ranks)	Hierarchical Observation
Organization of geneses	Time (mechanics)	Genetic	Time-table of exercises	Normalization
Control of activity	Body (anatomy)	Organic	Code of activities	Normalizing Judgment
Composition of forces	Society (economy)	Combinatory	Tactics	Alliances created Disciplinary Institution

and 'the dream of a perfect society', Foucault once more insists that it also developed a 'military dream of society', one organized not by ideas of nature, fundamental human rights and the social contract, but 'meticulously subordinated cogs of a machine', 'automatic docility' and 'permanent coercions' (169).

Here Foucault quotes Comte de Guibert (1743–1790), one of the great pre-Revolutionary theoreticians of military tactics, who argued for the need to create a national army and a plan for 'total war', based on the ideal of the Roman Republic/Empire, a linkage to which Foucault shortly returns. Foucault also draws attention to a letter from Marx that claims that the history of the military is important, since many features of modern capitalism and bourgeois society, like the division of labour, were taken initially from military procedures. We tend to celebrate the Enlightenment for its defence of public law and the ideal of the independent citizen that was promoted with the example of Rome, but Foucault reminds us of the other Roman aspect, the society based on a

double index: citizens and legionaries, law and manoeuvres. While jurists or philosophers were seeking in the pact a primal model for the construction or reconstruction of the social body, the soldiers and with them the technicians of discipline were elaborating procedures for the individual and collective coercion of bodies. (169)

Foucault now turns to the next section to describe the mechanisms of this new kind of bodily coercion.

2. The means of correct training

Unlike the older monarchical model of spectacular displays of power, discipline is a technique that tries not to draw attention to itself. Discipline works on a small scale; it operates at the level of individuals, not masses, and uses 'minor procedures' to create a 'calculated, but permanent economy' (170) of control. The three main instruments that it uses are: hierarchical observation, normalizing judgment and the combination of the two in the form of the examination.

Hierarchical observation coerces individuals by making them clearly visible and keeping them under watch. It works by constructing (architectural) space in ways that allow for total supervision, especially in ways where the viewer remains unseen by the viewed. Foucault's first example is the military camp that is formed in geometric lines for 'general visibility' (171). The layout of military camps was then carried into the design of cities, such as with the mid-nineteenth-century reconstruction of Paris's streets into long, straight boulevards, 'working-class housing estates, hospitals, asylums, prison, schools' (171), all sites where spaces could be embedded within one another for a telescopic viewpoint that provides 'an internal, articulated and detailed control' (172).

Architecture now begins to change so that buildings are made less to be seen from the outside, in order to achieve a monarch-like monumental appearance. Now they become constructed so as to organize their internal spaces for the benefit of those who will use observation to 'transform individuals' and 'make people docile and knowable' (172). Some examples of the latter are schoolrooms with doors that allow for passing teachers to look in the classroom at any time or eating halls with a table raised for the supervisors. 'These mechanism can only be seen as unimportant if one forgets the role of this instrumentation, minor but flawless, in the progressive objectification and the ever more subtle partitioning of individual behaviour' (173).

The 'perfect disciplinary apparatus' turns its building into a 'microscope of conduct', an 'apparatus of observation, recording and training' that would allow for a 'single gaze to see everything constantly' (173). The ideal building has a central point, where a 'perfect eye' could see all and to which everything had to turn for judging. The problem, however, is how to construct a building to create this kind of optical control. For this reason, circular architecture was often favoured at the time. For Foucault, this type of architecture became the expression of 'a certain political utopia' (174).

Yet the problem of visual organization was especially a challenge for the new large-scale industrial factories, where even a circle loses efficacy when it becomes too wide. The older manufactories had a system of inspectors from the outside who would come in and inspect. But as 'the machinery of production became larger and more complex, as the number of workers and the division of labour increased', there needed to be an internally regulating corps: a 'specialized personnel' of dedicated workers responsible for overseeing the process of production (174). Foucault argues that this 'new régime of surveillance' of manager-workers supervising the others was 'indissociable from the system of industrial production, private property and profit' (175), especially in buildings that were too large or crowded for a centralized observation post.

Foucault now quotes from Marx's *Capital* again on how 'directing, superintending and adjusting becomes one of the functions of capital' and '[o]nce a function of capital, it requires special characteristics' (175). The watching of labourers aims not only to make them docile, but also to make them more productive, more profit-producing.

New forms of internal managerial supervision, first developed in factories, were then introduced into schools, as students were chosen to monitor other students. 'Hierarchized, continuous and functional surveillance' (176) might not have been invented by the eighteenth century, but by making it part of an integrated system, the period turns observation into something like a machine itself. What is invidious about this optics is that because it only 'looks' but does not 'touch' the body, it seems to work outside of 'force or violence', even while it has a more subtle 'physical' control of people (177).

Foucault here illustrates his ideas of how this modern form of power works. Two aspects are particularly important: firstly, disciplinary power is a 'network of relations' that move 'from top to bottom, but also to a certain extent from bottom to top and laterally' (176). This is an important qualification that distinguishes Foucault's definition of modern power from those of other theoreticians who stress the repressive aspect of power 'from top to bottom'. Secondly, disciplinary power is 'not possessed as a thing'; rather, 'it functions like a piece of machinery' (177). Again, Foucault here departs from other concepts of power, especially in the marxist tradition, that see power as the 'property' of a particular group (e.g. the bourgeoisie), and replaces them with his notion of 'a relational power' that 'is everywhere and always alert' (177). Importantly, this definition of power is able to explain how individuals whose overall power may be limited can simultaneously be complicit in their own subjection and that of others. Foucault uses the spatial metaphor of the pyramid to suggest that modern power may have a 'head', but that individuals are distributed more widely in the field of power (177). The two different models might be visualized as such in Figure 3.1.

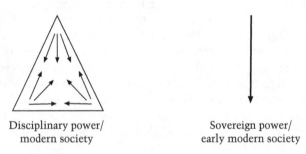

Disciplinary power/
modern society

Sovereign power/
early modern society

Figure 3.1

This control by sight emerges because of its linkage with a *normalizing judgment* (177), where individuals are simultaneously watched and evaluated. Once we enter an observed space, we become subject to a vision that seeks to ensure that we act well and follow certain kinds of behaviour. In this way, vision becomes the medium through which our actions can be constantly judged, not only for what we do that may break the rules, but also for how we fail to achieve a certain standard. The order we must follow is one that forces us to adapt to certain *norms*, more than simply obey regulations. This is a new kind of penality, an 'infra-penality' (178), which operates in areas not directly targeted by the law. Disciplinary institutions begin to operate through 'a whole micro-penality' that is aimed at activities, manners and sexual behaviour, speech and body posture (178). Disciplinary mechanisms also work through moments of petty humiliation; they seek to get inside us and make us fearful of being different.

In this way, 'disciplinary punishment' is *corrective* (179): it punishes us in order that we follow the models of behaviour, it is a kind of training device: 'To punish is to exercise' (180). This approach succeeds because it gives acts values involving clear oppositions of good and bad that are tied to a system of rewards and punishments where we might receive merits and demerits depending on our actions in relation to the norm.

This procedure brings together five distinct operations: it forces individuals to be compared against a larger group wherein they are differentiated according to their adherence to a rule; it makes this rule a minimum threshold, an average or optimal result which one should aim for (neither too far above or below this median); it uses numbers ('quantitative terms'), rather than descriptive accounts, to measure the ideal value of individuals; these numbers stand as rules that constrain behaviour; and it characterizes those who fail to conform, in either direction from the median, as 'abnormal' (183). 'The perpetual penality that traverses all points and supervises every instant in the disciplinary institutions compares, differentiates, hierarchizes, homogenizes, excludes. In short, it *normalizes*' (183).

Normalizing differs from prior historical systems of punishments, which had a fixed code of rules that must be remembered and followed; the new system is now much more plastic and mobile, since the norm is determined in relationship to an ever-changing hierarchy within the network of other people. We are judged not based on our own achievements or transgressions but in relationship to what everyone else is doing. In the prior system of social control, one, more or less, could avoid punishment by not committing proscribed acts; in the disciplinary model, one must be ever alert to how one's behaviour and personality exist in relationship to others. Whereas the older model punished illegal acts, the 'penality of the norm' measures 'the "nature" of individuals' (183); that is, disciplinary power constructs and targets *identities*, rather than acts.

This institutes a sort of constant paranoia where individuals can never stop comparing their actions and 'nature' to the perceived, or assumed, intangible norm. Yet because the group defining the norm is hard to see or comfortably know, since it is constantly fluid, we can never allow ourselves to rest in the secure knowledge that we have done the right thing. Since only the authority who can observe everyone is able to know what is the collective standard, we are left in a state of anxiety, wondering if our actions are sufficiently 'normal' or not. Are we eating too much or too little, for instance? Are our sexual desires acceptable or perverted? And so on. This uncertainty makes us more dependent on authorities, like doctors, teachers, etc. to tell us if our actions, personalities and bodies are normal or not. Additionally, we also begin to internalize the function of supervision, even in the absence of a supervisor, as we begin to interrogate our 'selves' to see if they are acceptably 'normal'.

Hence the undertow of observation not only allows for individuals to be graded and ranked, punished and rewarded, but it exerts a 'constant pressure to conform' (182) and enforces a desire to be normal. Yet disciplinary punishment

How to Read Foucault's *Discipline and Punish*

does not look to make the individual confess to their crimes, nor does it even seek to stop, or repress, bad acts. Instead it wants to *use* the presence of our being judged as potentially bad in relation to others (the failure to meet the norm) as a device for making people subordinate and harder working, more docile and useful.

This 'micro-economy of a perpetual penality' also means that because the individual is caught within ongoing reviews, a 'cycle of knowledge' about the individual is created (181); the individual now has a dossier, a genetic lifestory of his or her various deviations or adherence to a quantifiable norm. 'The power of the Norm' becomes more widespread and '[l]ike surveillance and with it, normalization becomes one the great instruments of power' in the modern period (184).

Foucault's examples are increasingly arguing for a similarity in different social institutions where the army ≈ courtroom ≈ school ≈ hospital ≈ prison ≈ factory. Today we might add the asylum or refugee camp to this list. As these disciplinary nodes constantly refer to each other and often collaborate, they create a network of control, with each centre radiating outward to blanket all aspects of society.

The creation of hierarchy through observation and a judgment about deviations from the norm becomes fused in the examination, in the dual sense of looking (to examine) and grading (by subjecting individuals to tests). The examination is discipline's ritual ceremony that establishes a 'truth' about the subject, a knowledge that will both give individuals a subjective identity through their ranked result and objectify them as things to be manoeuvred or exercised further.

Foucault argues that while attention has been paid to the development of the human sciences and its investigation into the signs and means of how we know things to be true, there has been little enquiry into 'what makes possible the knowledge that is transformed into political investment' (185). He describes this new use of information about individuals as a political device of control as an 'epistemological "thaw"' (185, the phrase also occurs 187, 191, 224). The metaphor of something solid slowly melting away is slightly unusual for Foucault, who is often associated with sharp clean breaks in social history. Instead, he uses the word 'thaw' to suggest that historical change is a slow process, full of multiple small stages, rather than one big break. The focus on the microscopic fits in here with his general argument that the noteworthy changes in the period's formations of power were energized through the deployment of small, seemingly inconsequential affairs.

He then gives some examples on how institutions change when they make the act of 'examining' routine. The first one is the hospital's transformation into an '"examining" apparatus' (185) as the physician's visits to patients became more regularized, scheduled and turned into a place of examining. Rather than a doctor appearing in times of emergency, like the priest, he comes more regularly, so that it seems as if the physician's job is constant supervision of the patient, rather than to intervene in crises. In a likewise fashion, the hospital became a training institution to educate other doctors, and this changed the nature of the building as it became a place of knowledge gathering, rather than simply one of physiological repair.

In the same way, the school 'became a sort of apparatus of uninterrupted examination' that 'enabled the teacher, while transmitting his knowledge, to transform his pupils into a whole field of knowledge' (186). In the pre-disciplinary age, an exam came at the end of training, like an apprenticeship, and once the test was passed, you were free from observation. Now, schools constantly examine their students, since exam rankings are seemingly more important as a process rather than as a final release from the teacher.

The exam is also a means for professionals based within institutions to assert their authority. The daily examining round of the physician displaces that of the 'unprofessional' priest. It also creates a knowledge (*savoir*), a medical discipline in the sense of what the doctor does and what she or he knows. The hospital, as institutional space, becomes 'the physical counterpart of the medical "discipline"' (186).

The examination as technique has three actions. Firstly, it '*transformed the economy of visibility into the exercise of power*' (187). Previously, to be seen was an empowering gesture. The monarch's spectacle of himself illustrated that he ought to be the centre of everyone's attention, since he was the source of all secular power. In the modern disciplinary age, to be seen is to be disempowered, where visibility is a sign of being subordinated to the examining eye. The examination is the 'ceremony' of an individual's 'objectification' (187).

Secondly, the examination brings individuals into '*the field of documentation*' (189); it registers them within a written dossier, where their performance and relative position to others can be tracked, compared and charted against the assumed norm. Indeed, the accumulation of dossiers provides the raw data to determine the numerical norm, as well. Once the 'constitution of the individual as a describable, analysable object' that can be looked at in terms of their personal development is achieved, there can be 'the constitution of a comparative system' that distributes people within a larger whole (190). These small techniques of arranging data about individuals were key to the creation of a 'science' about the individual.

Finally, the 'apparatus of writing' (190) within the examination-documentation complex makes each individual a 'case' (a history, a story of abnormality), a singular problem that 'has to be trained or corrected, classified, normalized, excluded, etc.' (191). Before the modern age, the ordinary individual was often 'below the threshold of description' (191) because the form of society was only interested in larger commemorative histories involving states, military conquest and important figures, like monarchs.

Disciplinary methods reversed this by making the very smallest social unit, the ordinary individual, a matter of great interest and fascination as 'a document for possible use' (191). When a person is now written about, it is not to make them seem heroic or worthy of public celebration and commemoration, instead it is to turn them into a case history, available only within the private circuits of professional evaluation. Consider how the people who have the biggest records on them are often the weakest in society; this documentation occurs because it is a 'procedure of objectification and subjectification' often visited on 'the child, the patient, the madman, the prisoner' (192).

In former times, the more one has power, the more one's life is documented by 'written accounts or visual reproductions' or named individually within a kinship group (193). This system was about 'ascending' individualization, where individual naming was praising of 'superior strength' (193). Discipline is about 'descending' individualization, where naming is incriminating – the more individualized one is in disciplinary records, the less powerful one has become.

For Foucault, this 'reversal of the procedures of individualization' is the precondition for the existence of '[a]ll sciences, analyses or practices employing the root "psycho-"' (193). The reversal of individualization results in the 'substituting for the individuality of the memorable man that of the calculable man' (193), and it is 'calculable man' who ultimately becomes the object of analysis for sciences like psychology or psychoanalysis.

Foucault here also comments on how this broader social shift was reflected in cultural forms or genres. In the Middle Ages, the chief cultural production was the adventure associated with the literary epic. In the modern age, it is the novel, the *Bildungsroman* (novel of development), with an 'internal search for childhood' (193). This turn from the 'noble deed to the secret singularity...from combats to phantasies' (193) belongs to the formation of disciplinary society and Foucault cites as an example the turn from the early modern Arthurian legends of the search for the visible Holy Grail to Freud's case histories about neurotics and their search for the hidden secret of their infantile sexuality. The medieval epic adventure is now replaced by the internal search for childhood, Le bon petit Henri becomes little Hans (the name Freud used for one of his patients); Lancelot becomes Judge Schreber (Freud's case study for paranoia). The older Romance tale of spiritual discovery through extramural conquest now becomes the Family Romance, Freud's name for the Oedipal saga, where an adult seeks to overcome their parents, rather than political Others.

Foucault once more cautions against limiting ourselves to the idea that individuality is a product only of mercantile capitalism's notion of society as a 'contractual association of isolated juridical subjects' (194). This political theory does require the production of individuals, but there was also a simultaneous 'technique for constituting individuals as...elements of power and knowledge' (194). Political and economic liberalism required the development of disciplinary techniques.

Foucault also insists that we should not think of 'the individual' as simply an 'ideological representation' or falsehood, since it is a 'reality fabricated by this specific technology of power' that he calls 'discipline' (194). He argues that we need to stop thinking in terms of power as a force that is negative, as something that 'excludes', 'represses', 'censors', 'abstracts', 'masks', or 'conceals' (a notion that Foucault calls the 'Repressive Hypothesis' in his next work, known in English as *The History of Sexuality: Volume I*). More succinctly, he simply states here that power 'produces reality; it produces domains of objects and rituals of truth. The individual and the knowledge that may be gained of him belong to this production' (194).

This is similar to his early claim that the exam, with its hierarchical surveillance and normalizing judgment, made possible the techniques of 'distribution and classification, maximum extraction of forces and time, continuous genetic accumulation, optimum combination of aptitudes and, thereby, the fabrication of cellular, organic, genetic and combinatory individuality' (192).

The notion that expressing our individuality is a feature of our weakness, rather than our strength, will be surprising to many. Foucault radically implies that the politics of personal identity, from the late 1960s onward, was a mistake, given that in the modern system of discipline,

How to Read Foucault's *Discipline and Punish*

we could say that to be marked as having an identity is a feature of disempowerment. It might be worth considering this claim in relation to the new social networks, where people display their likes and dislikes on the internet. Does not this invite others to judge, and implicitly normalize, us? By laying bare and constantly recording our personalities, are we not complicit in our own imprisonment?

Having charted out the techniques of discipline, Foucault concludes this section by asking how it was that power could achieve such effects, and he will move onward to illustrate how a certain practice managed to achieve the effects that it sought to accomplish.

3. Panopticism

This section is surely the most familiar one for readers who know *Discipline and Punish* from anthologies. Interestingly, it is also the section that is most clearly based on English language materials and the one with illustrations that display Foucault's point more cogently than the other plates included with *Discipline and Punish*. The ease in which this section achieves clarity, however, has often been at the expense of the rest of Foucault's historical and political argument. When reading it, be sure to contextualize its claims within the rest of Foucault's argument.

Foucault begins by contrasting the plague town with the leper colony. The plague town is modern-looking as it quarantines people by dividing space into gridded partitions that are constantly watched by officials for movements in, out and within. This surveillance is also based on a system of documentation and registration of who has become ill. By enclosing, segmenting, observing, evaluating and documenting the isolated space, the plague town 'constitutes a compact model of the disciplinary mechanism' (197). While there is the 'literary fiction' (197) of the plague town as a festival-like time and space when restrictions were lifted, with liberty to live more freely or escape from the oversight of authorities and compulsion to work, Foucault argues that there was also the total opposite, when 'even the smallest details of everyday life' were organized by power – a 'capillary' power that penetrated the most intricate areas of each person's life (198).

The leper colony was more simply a matter of exclusion, of dumping individuals into an enclosed space of permanent exile in order, essentially, to make them unseen and forgotten. Against the physically marked leper's exclusion through confinement, the plague city's segmentation and its distributions and analysis stands as an entirely different model of social organization and correct training. The leper colony was a 'pure community' of aliens, while the plague town was a 'disciplined society' (198) that enclosed people within a dossier of knowledge gathering. These spaces have two entirely different ways of exercising power. Leper-town is where an Other is repressively ostracized and *excluded*, while the plague city organizes illness and functions as a means of social *inclusion*, where people must constantly examine themselves for the presence of illness and then 'produce' their normality (in this case, lack of disease) for viewing authorities.

Yet Foucault says that the gestures within these different projects come 'slowly together' in the nineteenth century as the space of exclusion and 'the technique of power proper to disciplinary partitioning' (199) – leper colony and plague town – merge and become applied within institutions such as 'the psychiatric asylum, the penitentiary, the reformatory, the approved school and, to some extent, the hospital' (199). In these institutions, authorities had control over individuals whom they could differentiate through tactics of binary division ('mad/sane; dangerous/harmless; normal/abnormal', 199) and coercive assignment, where people are distributed according to evaluations, which will determine what they must do. In this way, individuals are both excluded and included through constant, individualizing examination – they are 'brand[ed]' and 'alter[ed]' at the same time (199).

Foucault now turns to describe English utilitarian philosopher Jeremy Bentham's plan for a privatized prison, *Panopticon: or, the Inspection-House* (1787). In this, Bentham (1742–1836) described the use of architecture to enable inspection for prisons, workhouses, factories, insane asylums, hospitals and schools. Foucault here gives a relatively documentary account of what Bentham proposes for the ideal prison's construction. The prison should be a circular building with a central watchtower. Around this will be cells that are backlit with a window, allowing light to flow in and through the cell so as to make the prisoner visible to anyone looking from within the prison. In this way, a guard in the tower can observe the cells, the inhabitants of which will never know if they are being watched or not, since the tower's watchroom is either cast in shadows or visually obstructed. If traditional prisons meant to enclose prisoners and hide them without light, Bentham's only seeks to enclose them, but this time in full view where they can be controlled by surveillance. In this scheme, '[v]isibility is a trap' (200). The Panopticon thus both automates and deindividualizes the functioning of power, especially as it no longer matters who is in the central tower, or even if there is anyone at all. The prison becomes much cheaper and more efficient to run as it relies on the prisoner's sense of being watched, rather than being threatened with physical force. While the King's terror required the expense of a public ritual and guards, the Panopticon's discipline only requires the prison's silent architecture.

By isolating every individual in their own cell, the Panopticon breaks up the possibility of prisoners forming (rebellious) collectives, and it turns every prisoner into 'the object of information, never a subject in communication' (200). Yet the Panopticon's 'major effect' is 'to induce in the inmate a state of conscious and permanent visibility that assures the automatic functioning of power' (201). Because a prisoner can never know if she or he is being watched, the prisoner thus 'becomes the principle of [their] own subjection' (203) as they constantly police their behaviour in the fear that they might be observed at any time.

Like a zoo, the Panopticon also allows for its subjects to be differentiated into different categories or nomenclature classifications. Furthermore, it functions as a laboratory that can change behaviour and 'train or correct individuals' (203) by allowing authorities to try out different punishments and analyse how successful they have functioned. As a place for 'experiments on men', a 'laboratory of power' (204), the Panopticon even captures guards within its grasp, as it allows for the inspectors to themselves be inspected, thus destroying the barrier between the empowered and the disempowered.

If the plague town's discipline appears only as an exceptional state in times of emergency, against an 'extraordinary evil', the panoptic principle is a generalized state 'in the everyday life of men' (205). Because it only needs a certain architecture to achieve its effects, Bentham argues that the Panopticon can be used on subjects other than merely prisoners; its method works on hospital patients, schoolchildren, workers and psychiatric patients. As Bentham describes it: '"Morals reformed – health preserved – industry invigorated – instruction diffused – public burthens lightened...all by a simple idea in architecture!"' (207). Once this idea of the observational apparatus appeared, it was easily integrated through different institutions – 'education, medical treatment, production, punishment' (206) – and spread very quickly throughout society. The Panopticon can thus be introduced to proliferate discipline in 'the very foundations of society' (208) as a 'procedure of subordination of bodies and forces that must increase the utility of power' while dispensing with the need for a central authority, like the monarch (208).

Bentham's idea became attractive since it helped to address the need for an inexpensive mechanism to increase power over larger populations and control over popular rebellions. Unlike the older monarch, who sought to impress through terrific spectacle, the Panopticon shows that disciplinary power is more productive if it works surreptitiously and through small details involving space, time and normalizing evaluations. Bentham's project relies on 'the capillary functioning of power' (198) that can do without a central authority, while facilitating power relations to spread throughout society, by means of its small arteries and veins. The Panopticon even appears as superficially democratic, since everyone, prisoners and guards, seems to be equally bound up within its optics.

The 'Benthamite physics of power' (209) had operated earlier in European history, but it proposes a noteworthy historical transformation by encouraging that disciplinary techniques are spread out far more widely than they had ever done before. It proposes this extension through three processes.

The first is the *functional inversion of disciplines'* (210) wherein institutions are now asked to produce, rather than repress, social phenomena. Discipline is not simply a negative means of neutralizing dangers or of controlling floating populations; it does not look at people only to prevent them from doing things. While it seeks to stop desertions from the military, workplace theft, or schoolchildren skipping classes, discipline is significantly combined with a moral and physical training that aims to create 'useful individuals' (211), especially for factories and armies.

The second process involves the *'swarming of disciplinary mechanisms'* (211). Various different institutions begin to act like one another and collaborate in order to form a coherent whole achieved by the convergence of smaller disciplinary nodes. Not only do schools, hospitals and prisons increasingly operate like one another, they are also used as 'centres of observation disseminated throughout society' (212) to form a network of surveillance not only of those within their walls, but crucially the population outside them as well (e.g. the homes and parents of schoolchildren). These institutions' authorities increasingly became more confident that they have the right to go into public spheres and spaces that would have previously been thought 'private' and free from interference by inspectors. Not only is the private space of the home, and all its (gendered) activities, penetrated by these authorities, but, increasingly, the private mind of the occupants, their behavioural morality and socialization, become the target of approval.

The third process is the '*state-control of the mechanisms of discipline*' (213). A centralized police apparatus develops that becomes involved with these different institutions so that the State can exercise surveillance on the population through communication with these different disciplinary apparatuses. Expanding on its role under royal absolutism, the police 'added a disciplinary function to its role as the auxiliary of justice in the pursuit of criminals and as an instrument for the political supervision of plots, opposition movements or revolts' (214–15). The police, supported by 'its armed force', now intervened where the 'enclosed institutions of discipline (workshops, armies, schools)' reached their limit, 'disciplining the non-disciplinary spaces' (215).

Foucault, though, insists that discipline should not be linked to a *specific* institution or (state) apparatus, since it is a 'type of power, a modality for its exercise, compromising a whole set of instruments, techniques, procedures, levels of application, targets; it is a "physics" or an "anatomy" of power, a technology' (215). This new type of power is used by institutions (like prisons), authorities (in schools or hospitals) and state apparatuses 'whose major, if not exclusive, function is to assure that discipline reigns over society as a whole (the police)' (216). If we can easily speak of a disciplinary society, it is only because these techniques have been invested within and act as a linking device for several agencies, professionals and state bureaucracies.

Here Foucault repeats some of the earlier arguments as he contrasts a society of the spectacle to one of surveillance, and he argues that we descend today less from classical

(Greek) society than the Napoleonic Empire in this regard. Unlike the great spectacles of Antiquity, with its intensity and sensuality of public life, the modern age is more inward looking and works on individuals, rather than crowds, although every individual is caught under the blanket of observation.

The formation of a disciplinary society connects with a set of broader historical processes, three of which Foucault highlights: one economic, another juridical and political and the third scientific.

Firstly, the 'disciplines are techniques for assuring the ordering of human multiplicities' (218) in ways that reduce the cost, both financially and politically, of their operation; intensify their effects while also broadening them; and increase the docility and utility of those subjected to their (educational, military, industrial or medical) institutions. Discipline works because it is a technique for dealing with multiplicities cheaply (economic); it maximizes intensity (juridico-political); and links economic growth to apparatuses.

The 'triple objective of the disciplines' (218) corresponds to the needs of the bourgeois-aligned social classes who were concerned about the effects of two historical developments. The first was a general concern about the increasing population, from the second half of the eighteenth century, and a specific one about the large numbers of displaced peasants and urban workers alongside an increase in those who had been placed inside certain kinds of institutions (the growth of schools, the emergence of a mass army, the increase of patients in hospitals). Demographic growth of an increased labouring class population created a floating (unemployed) population that was potentially threatening to the middle class. How could this undifferentiated and mobile mass be controlled and turned into a force of productive labourers?

The second concern was over the management of the new production processes within capitalist-oriented factories that constantly needed to increase their profit. The older forms of organizing production from the feudal and monarchical period were no longer capable of responding to the explosive growth created by new technologies and work conditions. Instruments of production (i.e. industrialization, but also a more complex State) were becoming more complicated. The question was how to manage these processes more profitably in ways that would prevent the system from self-destructing.

To overcome the older 'economy of power' (219), the social interests that promoted the use of discipline had to solve a number of problems. Initially they had to solve the riddle of the 'inefficiency of mass phenomena', as larger groups were often less productive than traditional ones. Consequently, there had to be a means for breaking up masses and calculating new ways for people to be segmented and distributed. Disciplinary interests thus had to master the forces of an 'organized multiplicity', while also neutralizing the 'counter-power that springs from them and which form a resistance to the power that wishes to dominate: agitations, revolts, spontaneous organizations, coalitions – anything that may establish horizontal conjunctions' (219). To prevent these horizontal linkages, discipline both partitions and makes hierarchizing distinctions to scramble any possible social connections among the lower classes, while also increasing the efficiency of these smaller units by means of 'hierarchical surveillance, continuous registration, perpetual assessment and classification' (220). Additionally, the forces of discipline have to bring in these new power relations discreetly, in ways that do not arouse suspicions among those being controlled. Or, as Foucault says, 'the disciplines are the ensemble of minute technical inventions that made it possible to increase the useful size of multiplicities by decreasing the inconveniences of the power which, in order to make them useful, must control them' (220).

The chief influence here involves the intermixture of disciplinary techniques for the 'accumulation of capital' with those for 'administering the accumulation of men' (220). These two processes of capitalist exploitation and discipline 'cannot be separated; it would not have been possible to solve' one problem without the other (221) (Foucault here again draws on Marx's *Capital* at this point). Capitalism and discipline are directly related: '[e]ach makes the other possible and necessary; each provides a model for the other' (221). The 'growth of a capitalist economy gave rise to the specific modality of disciplinary power'; it is a power that 'could be operated in the most diverse political régimes, apparatuses or institutions' (221).

The second historical process after capitalism that is significant for the introduction of discipline is the growth of bourgeois civil society and its mythology of a 'formally egalitarian juridical framework' and 'parliamentary, representative régime' (222). It was possible to guarantee 'a system of rights that were egalitarian in principle' for a mass citizenry only because of the development of 'systems of micro-power that are essentially non-egalitarian' (222). That is, disciplinary mechanisms are needed to ensure that these citizens will be made submissive within a system that appears to be one of equal rights and organized by consensual contracts. Foucault here draws attention to a 'dark side' behind the egalitarian rhetoric: 'The "Enlightenment", which discovered the liberties, also invented the disciplines' (222). If democratic or republican society appears to distribute power more widely among the lower classes, this was possible only because discipline covertly removes this power from them.

Foucault argues that the middle class had to come up with a system that seemed fair, rational and equalizing in order to overthrow the aristocratic and monarchical society, but they did not actually want to form a society in which they could not dominate the lower classes. So, while the middle class promoted a language of rights, these were meant only for their own use, while the action of discipline was directed, surreptitiously, to the labouring classes as an 'infra-law' and 'counter-law' against the public 'law' of equality (222). Discipline acts as a protective counter-weight to the law of equality because it creates a relationship between individuals that involves constraints that are 'entirely different from contractual obligation' (222), since these constraints are structurally created for the 'non-reversible subordination of one group of people by another' (222–3), namely the subordination of the lower classes to the bourgeoisie.

The rise of capitalism and bourgeois civil society are the first two processes responsible for the success of discipline, but there is also a third one, which involves the emergence and development of the 'human' sciences, like psychology, psychiatry, pedagogy and criminology, where the branches of knowledge crossed a unique threshold in the eighteenth century. While the scientific advances of the period are well documented, because they often correspond to academic subjects, Foucault argues that discipline and its related knowledge production is as important as the others. He considers the inquisitorial juridical investigations in the Middle Ages as akin to the 'birth of the states and of monarchical sovereignty' as well as early empiricism (225). A similar correlation occurs in the modern period with the 'sciences of man' and the rise of civil society and a capitalist economy. If the public execution was the 'logical culmination of a procedure governed by the Inquisition', then the 'practice of placing individuals under "observation" is a natural extension of a justice imbued with disciplinary methods and examination procedures' (227). Modern penality is characterized by efforts to problematize the criminal's personality, more than the crime itself; the concern to punish in a way that will be a 'correction, a therapy, a normalization' of this personality; and the division of judgment among 'various authorities that are supposed to measure, assess, diagnose, cure, transform individuals' (227). But these disciplinary techniques are not limited to prison alone, as they are taken up and distributed throughout society by similar kinds of institutions and their 'experts in normality, who continue and multiply the functions of the judge' (228). Hence, Foucault ends by asking: 'Is it surprising that prisons resemble factories, schools, barracks, hospitals, which all resemble prisons' (228)?

At this point, it might help to review by a table the differences between the terror of the *Ancien Régime* and modern discipline (Table 3.3). Keep in mind that the table leaves out the second, intermediary phase of punishment for the sake of emphasis.

Table 3.3

Torture	Discipline
Ancien Régime (early modern)	Modernity
External punishment	Internalized punishment
Disfigured body	Docile body, the 'soul'
Main site is scaffold (public 'ceremony of pain')	Main site is prison ('secrecy of administration')
Spectacle	Surveillance
Punishment occurs at one concentrated point	Punishment happens in multiple nodes
Terror – punishment is atrocious	Humanism – punishment is gentle
Punishment is enacted by:	Punishment is enacted by:
Shameless Punisher	Ashamed System
(King-executioner proudly displays body to crowd)	(several 'experts' distribute responsibility)
The criminal **act** is punished	The criminal **identity** is punished/ reformed
Private Trial/Public Punishment	Public Trial/Private Punishment
The confession must be repeated	The dossier is to be repeated
(The subject speaks)	(The subject is spoken about)
Point of penality: stop popular resistance by repression	Point of penality: stop popular resistance by producing personality
Punishment can be ended by:	Punishment can be ended by:
The King's Lenient Pardon of the Criminal	Society's Therapeutic Cure of the Criminal
Crime is represented as an:	Crime is represented as an:
attack against the King's body as natural and eternal	attack against civil society (property/labour contract as social contract)
Crime against authority	Crime against property
Penality organized by the Paternal King	Penality organized by the middle class
Visibility is a sign of authority	Visibility is a sign of abnormality
Juridical investigation	Disciplinary examination
Status	Class

Part Four: Prison

1. Complete and austere institutions

After having charted out the three ages of penal justice, Foucault turns now to focus on the prison, as the new material apparatus of the modern disciplinary system in the last years of the eighteenth century and early to mid nineteenth century. He begins by acknowledging that we might wonder what was so new about prisons, since prisons predate the disciplinary techniques that are '[t]he general form of an apparatus intended to render individuals docile and useful, by means of precise work on their bodies' (231). Remember that these techniques involve:

> distributing individuals, fixing them in space, classifying them, extracting from them the maximum in time and forces, training their bodies, coding their continuous behaviour, maintaining them in perfect visibility, forming around them an apparatus of observation, registration and recording, constituting on them a body of knowledge that is accumulated and centralized. (231)

Yet the question remains: why did detention become the standard punishment for all crimes? The new 'model' prisons – Ghent, Gloucester, Walnut Street – are the 'first visible points of this transition', as they relate to the fusion of prison and the human sciences, but Foucault significantly does not consider them entirely new 'innovations' or periodizing events (231). Foucault insists, instead, that the significant turn in the history of the prison is its implementation in an overall 'history of [those] disciplinary mechanisms that the new [bourgeois] class power was developing...in which they colonized the legal institution' (231). This moment in history saw the strategic use of a rhetoric of 'human' treatment and the fiction of the contract. Foucault argues that the emerging middle class developed a new way of understanding punishment that appears to be 'equal', but is actually unfair, with 'all the asymmetries of disciplinary subjection' (232), where asymmetry means social inequality.

Prison seems a self-evident and logical method of punishment, without any easy alternatives, but this is only because we exist in a society controlled by the middle class that celebrates individual liberty as the universal feature of equality. In this perspective, if everyone, rich and poor, has a natural right to liberty, then removing personal freedom 'must' be the most fair and equal punishment, unlike fines, which the wealthy can pay with less bother. Additionally, prison time places a value on segmented time, making it like the form of wages and aligning it with the rise of an economic system that pays labourers for their time, rather than the objects they produce. This economic language appears in the cliché that one is in prison to 'pay's one debt' (233) to society. Hence, the prison becomes 'natural' to us just as it seems 'natural' to use time to measure exchanges in wages. If everyone is 'equal' before the law, according to the ideology of the individual free to trade and sell in the marketplace, then what could be a more appropriate and egalitarian gesture than to deny someone their individual freedom to act as a commercial agent, to buy and to sell labour and time? This type of punishment turns time and space into units of 'life' currency that can be traded.

From the perspective of middle-class ideology, wherein there is no such thing as society, just individual self-interest, if detention seems a 'self-evident' punishment to us, it is because we have internalized the presuppositions of the individual's right to act alone in the marketplace as greater than collective or social concerns.

Yet the 'deprivation of liberty' in prison was also tied from the beginning of the nineteenth century to 'the technical transformation of individuals' (233). In other words, time in prison is not just a matter of payment for social damage, prison is also primarily considered as a corrective institution, one that means to change the prisoner, to reform her or him. Seeking to make the prison a 'complete and austere institution' (the section's title quotes prison architect Louis Pierre Baltard [1764–1846]), which took over every aspect of the prisoner's life, prison administrators wanted it to be 'omni-disciplinary', a means of 'recoding [the prisoner's] existence', a house of correction (236).

With this turn to techniques of correction, prisons became reformatories, engines that transform humans. In order to achieve 'almost total power over the prisoners' (236), the prison reformers believed in 'three great schemata: the politico-moral schema of individual isolation and hierarchy; the economic model of force applied to compulsory work; the technico-medical model of cure and normalization. The cell, the workshop, the hospital' (248).

The first of these schemes insisted that prisoners be isolated so that maximum force could be applied to him or her. The idea that the prisoner should be separated from contact with the outside world was carried even further to isolate individuals from each other inside prison. Segmenting prisoners into personal cells was partly to prevent plots and revolts from being hatched, but it also emerges from the proclaimed idea that remorse for the crime can only come if the prisoner is forced to reflect on himself alone. Lastly, isolation also makes prisoners docile as they become dependent on prison guards and administrators for their wellbeing, rather than the network of other prisoners.

In the actual implementation of isolation, there was a debate between two American model prisons. Auburn in New York allowed prisoners to work and eat in common, although they were only allowed to address the warders. The Philadelphia system kept the prisoner in total isolation. But whatever system was used, the purpose was to use isolation as a means of 'coercive individualization' (239).

The second aspect of the penitentiary involves making prisoners work, where labour was considered 'with isolation, as an agent of carceral transformation' (240). The matter of prison work was, however, contested. There was a debate during the July Monarchy (1830–1848) about paying prisoners for their work, especially because paid work did not automatically guarantee moral reformation. Workers outside the prison were opposed to prisoners making commodities for sale, since competition from lower-paid prisoners undermined the struggles of regular labourers for fair wages. Urban workers also complained that prisoners got to work with their housing and food secured, while urban labourers did not (thus forcing the latter to accept lower wages in their desperation to get any kind of money for basic life needs or, in the worst case, driving free labourers into crime or prostitution).

Prison authorities were generally unsympathetic to complaints by labourers, insisting that prison labour was necessary as a 'principle of order and regularity' (242) within the institution as it helped to create opportunities for installing hierarchy and surveillance. Foucault similarly argues that prison labour was never meant to be profitable or train someone in skills, but simply to make them submissive within the prison and teach them to adjust to labour conditions outside of the prison. Authorities felt that 'prison is not a workshop' in which convicts worked; it was a 'machine whose convict-workers are both the cogs and the products' (242). Prison factories produced commodities, but they also transformed individuals, who had been 'mechanized according to the general norms of an industrial society' (242), and prepared them for a future as docile workers in industrial factories. The goal was not only '[t]he making of machine-men, but also of proletarians' (242).

Consequently, when wages are given in the prison, it is not to remunerate labour, but to 'function as a motive and measure of individual transformation'; it is not a contract between employer and employee, but a technique of 'correction' (243). Foucault then goes one step further as he ultimately claims that the real purpose of penal labour is not to create profit by underpaying prisoners for the goods they make, nor even to train prisoners in employable skills, but to constitute a new 'power relation' through an 'empty economic form' (the small wages) and the individual's submission and 'adjustment to a production apparatus' (243). The chief purpose is to establish a new means of long-term control over the prisoner's life, even beyond simply fixing her or him to the new capitalist economies. Thus, Foucault ends this section with one of the rare instances of his recognition of women, by quoting the account of a women's prison working quietly in contrast to the '"disorder of ideas and morals"' (244) outside the institution in order to emphasize that the main concern here is to change individuals' morality, attitude and personality, as realms that go beyond simple submission within the factory.

It is this notion of changing the personality of the prisoner that involves the third penal element: the idea that the length and nature of the prison sentence should not be solely determined by the nature of the crime, but is to be modulated according to the prisoner's performance within the prison, his or her ability to demonstrate good behaviour. The prison is the space where individuals are pressured to cure themselves of criminal desires and display their rescue by acting in ways that would warrant discharge from the hospital-like prison. In this focus on altering the length of a prison sentence by what occurs inside prisons, there is a significant shift then in the power over the prisoner from the judge to prison administrators, who now have the authority to individualize and vary the length of the sentence. Foucault calls this the 'Declaration of Carceral Independence' (247) or a new 'punitive sovereignty' where the prison officials become more independent and autonomous; they leap over the sentencing judge and assume a monarchical-like power over the prisoner, but a power gained over the prisoner through mechanisms of observation, diagnosis, characterization and classifying information.

Having described the interconnection of isolation, compulsory work and the therapeutic value of variable sentences, Foucault can now characterize the modern prison as a 'penitentiary', a place where 'techniques of a disciplinary type' (248) have been added to traditional detention with its sole purpose of momentary enclosure of the accused. 'The margin by which the prison exceeds detention is filled in fact by techniques of a disciplinary type. And this disciplinary addition to the juridical is what, in short, is called, "the penitentiary"' (248).

Watch how Foucault uses his terminology in service of his argument. As mentioned, he is not arguing that prisons, in themselves, are new. Instead he is claiming that when the architecture of prisons and imprisonment as punishment were matched with disciplinary techniques and social class interests, the prison became the 'penitentiary'.

Detention + (disciplinary techniques: isolation + forced labour + moral reform) = the Penitentiary

This turn to the penitentiary did not come without it being contested by judges, for instance, who were not so willing to yield control to prison warders. Yet ultimately judges were not able to resist the way in which the prison was able to combine surveillance with a 'clinical knowledge about the convicts' (249) through observation. By the 1830s, Bentham's theoretical treatise on the Panopticon's procedures had become reality as many prisons began to be organized in this fashion, turning them into a 'prison-machine' for individualizing observation and permanent documentation.

The combination of disciplinary techniques with a behavioural dossier leads Foucault to his real argument about what differentiates the modern prison from prior ones.

The fusion of discipline with registration allows prisons to become the place where a new subjective identity is produced out of offenders: the delinquent. Penitentiaries, with all their apparatus of observation and evaluation, accept an *offender* from the judge and deliver back a *delinquent*, 'the offender becomes an individual to know' (251) beyond the prison's walls.

While an offender is someone who has committed a criminal *act* that needs to be punished in a repressive manner (the removal of individual liberty, for instance), a delinquent is someone with an *identity* that can now be subjected to a 'biographical knowledge and a technique for correcting individual lives' (252), where the delinquent's entire life, even before the committed crime, is open to evaluation. The 'biographical' is important to the history of penal justice since it 'establishes the "criminal" as existing even before the crime and even outside it' (252). It allows the criminal to be examined 'from the triple point of view of psychology, social position and upbringing, in order to discover the dangerous proclivities of the first, the harmful dispositions of the second and the bad antecedents of the third' (252). The behavioural dossier acts as a retrospective prophecy by detailing an individual's traits as the cause of the crime. It creates a 'criminal personality' even before the individual broke any law or committed any crime at all. '[P]enal discourse and psychiatric discourse' (252) cross each other's paths as they create the category of a 'criminal personality' that allows for authorities to proclaim a causal history of crime outside of the prison. 'The penitentiary technique and the delinquent are in a sense twin brothers' (255) because this pairing allows prison authorities to overcome the authority of the judge and link up with other kinds of institutional authorities, like social workers or psychiatrists. 'Delinquency is the vengeance of the prison on justice' (255), as it enables the prison to liberate itself from the court system and form alliances with a host of other bureaucratic agencies, whose rules are rarely seen or authorized by the citizenry. In this way, a social infrastructure emerges that might as well be invisible. Foucault calls this an infrapower because it is different from the more easily seen outside structure of the State and its legal, political and police realms.

As the delinquent allows for the treatment of a host of aspects involving the prisoners' instincts, drives and tendencies, his or her character is explained as the result of belonging to 'quasi-natural classes'; the prison becomes a base for an 'ethnography of crime' that gradually develops into 'a systematic typology of delinquents' (253). By classifying different kinds of criminal personalities, each of which would be given different kinds of treatments within the prison, prison authorities assemble a 'scientific' knowledge that distinguishes the prisoner from the tortured body or one simply deprived of liberty. The greater purpose in making a convict (someone who has broken the law) into a 'delinquent' (a law-breaker that can be 'reformed') is that it allows prison officials to examine the individual's biography to see where things went wrong, and, by investigating the individual's background, it is possible to create a quasi-animal classification of social types and their hierarchy within a criminal milieu. By analysing the delinquent, you can judge the background context of their birth, adolescence and community relations. Hence the real target of 'reform' is the criminal's social class, i.e. the restive labouring classes (that were known in the mid nineteenth century as the 'dangerous classes'), which authorities now condemn as deviant in ways that seem to be innocent of any explicit class prejudice. The working classes are not seen as an economic group, but as a cultural one that can be more easily shaped.

From the eighteenth century, there were two different ways to objectify criminals. One could see them as 'monsters' that had broken away from the social pact. The other was to see them as 'juridical subject[s] rehabilitated by punishment' (256). The difference between these two modes was resolved as the penitentiary, conjoining medicine, psychology and criminology, manufactured the 'delinquent' as 'object' from which a criminological 'truth' can be produced about individuals and their society, both of which are contaminated, but curable (256). As the prison becomes a generator of knowledge, we can now turn to see what value this knowledge-product (the delinquent) has for bourgeois society.

By elaborating a truth about the abnormal delinquent, the penitentiary could, by extension, serve as a means for labelling a social class, the working class, as abnormal because they have not accepted the normal behaviour and rule of middle-class society. Foucault argues that the ideas of the Enlightenment prison reformers or even those of Bentham cannot explain the ubiquity of imprisonment; the rise of the 'prison came from elsewhere – from the mechanisms proper to a disciplinary power' (256) and the social interests deploying this power as a strategy.

It is this creation of the abnormal, knowable individual that is the actual goal of the modern prison and the justification for its expense. 'As a highly efficient technology, penitentiary practice produces a return on the capital invested in the penal system and in the building of heavy prisons' (251). The utility of delinquency for middle-class society is Foucault's theme in the next section. For Foucault, any history of ideas needs to be rooted in a history of socioeconomic conflicts (and vice-versa).

2. Illegalities and delinquency

From the law's perspective, detention is simply the removal of liberty, individual freedom. But within a system organized according to disciplinary purposes, imprisonment serves a very different purpose, especially when it means to reform individuals. A key moment in this transition, for Foucault, comes in 1837 with the replacement of the chain-gang, where prisoners were still seen in public, by the prison carriage, where prisoners were carried from one place to another in a carriage that could not be seen by outsiders.

The chain-gang was stopped by state authorities as it became increasingly dangerous to parade it through the streets, because these processions were opportunities for rowdy spectatorship by the lower classes. As time went on, the chain-gang's processional served as an opportunity to enjoy the display of the prisoners as noxious items or as elements in a game of physiognomy (where one tried to guess the crime from the face), both of which the convicts learned to play up to in ways similar to those of professional wrestling's masquerades of super-villains: 'As they passed, they mimed the scenes of their crimes, mocking the judges or the police, boasting of as yet undiscovered deeds of wickedness' (260).

The chain-gangs turned from 'a penalty' into a 'privilege' as they developed into carnivals, with the prisoners using the public moment less as a place to show repentance and more as a possibility for the 'mad joy' of mocking authority by serenading themselves (261). By inverting the hierarchy and presenting their punishment as an invitation to a pleasure jaunt, like a May-day picnic, the prisoners intimated the presence of a new spirit among the working classes, a spirit of revolutionary rebellion (a 'political Sabbath', 261). The songs that the criminals sang in the gang presented a 'new tonality' in which the judgments of the court were rejected and their moral legitimacy questioned (262). The restive spirit of the criminals in the chain-gang thus gave 'a kind of symbolic outlet' (262) for the expression of lower-class resentments, where the convicts were seen as unfairly treated comrades rather than public enemies. Crowds increasingly came to watch the chain-gang's frolics as a safe way of themselves mocking the authorities.

Because of the popular support for criminals during their public promenades, the chain-gang was quickly replaced with the enclosed prison carriage, where there would no longer be any contact between convict and public. In the sealed carriage, the convicts had to be silent as they were observed by guards, in what was in essence a disciplinary mini-prison, 'a mobile equivalent of the Panopticon' (263).

Foucault then turns to a topic that allows him to clearly establish connections between the historical material and his own contemporary moment, the late twentieth century. He discusses how the prison was recognized almost from its start as a failure, and he lists six longstanding complaints about prisons. Prisons do not lower the crime rate; instead they multiply the kinds of things that cause crime, even as the number of criminals remains about the same. Prisons cause recidivism. Released convicts simply get caught again and return to prison. Prison produces delinquents, or recidivist criminals, because it instils within prisoners a feeling of resentment against the 'arbitrary power of administration' (266), and the released prisoner is thus more likely to want to seek revenge by committing more crimes. This revenge is made possible, as prison creates a culture and 'milieu of delinquents, loyal to one another, hierarchized, ready to aid and abet any future criminal act' (267); it is a university of crime. The ex-criminal finds it difficult to leave a life of crime, even if he or she wants to, because it is difficult to overcome the stigma of imprisonment. Ex-convicts are frequently unable to find work or stable housing and so almost inevitably drift back to a life of crime. Finally, 'prison indirectly produces delinquents by throwing the inmate's family into destitution' (268) as the (often) male earner is absent, forcing the other family members into impoverishment, and this means that other family members might turn to crime from desperation.

These complaints about prison might make it seem that prison simply needs to be more effective, more corrective and run more cheaply. Inevitably, though, the answer to these problems is more prison. 'For a century and a half the prison had always been offered as its own remedy: the reactivation of the penitentiary techniques as the only means of overcoming their perpetual failure' (268).

To prove this point, Foucault cites the responses to the French prison uprisings between 1972 and 1974 that reiterated the need for the traditional 'seven universal maxims of the good "penitential condition"' (269): prison must transform the individual's behaviour (*correction*); convicts must be either isolated or distributed according to their act (*classification*); prison sentences must be able to be altered based on the convict's behaviour (*modulation of penalties*); work must be 'one of the essential elements in the transformation and progressive socialization of convicts' (269), (*work as obligation and right*); education, similarly, is an obligation (*penitentiary education*); the prison must have its own specialized staff of supervisors and administrators who can morally 'educate' the convicts (*technical supervision of detention*); and post-release prisoners must be followed up with continued supervision, like parole officers (*auxiliary institutions*).

Foucault notes that '[w]ord for word, from one century to the other, the same fundamental propositions are repeated' (270). Because of this lack of change, he argues that it is wrong to think of the prison in terms of several phases of prison reform. Instead, he believes that almost from the start, there has been a simultaneous appearance of four elements alongside prison's removal of individual liberty. These elements are the introduction of a disciplinary 'super-power' through architecture (exemplified by the panoptical eye of supervision); 'auxiliary knowledge' where the prison is used as a device to create knowledge of the prisoner by means of 'coercive regulations and scientific propositions'; 'inverted efficiency', where prison creates the very delinquency which it is supposed to remove; and 'utopian duplication', in which the practices of rehabilitating prisoners and reforming the prison institution repeat the ones of discipline (271).

Foucault here insists that because of the repetition of these age-old complaints about prison, we should not think of prison as a failure, which has been reformed in ensuing stages. Rather we should accept that prison's 'supposed failure' is, in fact, its true function (271). The 'model prison' that opened in 1969 has the same architectural shape as the one in 1836, because, as Foucault argues in one of his most stunning claims, the strategic purpose of prison is to *produce* 'illegalities and delinquency' or, more precisely to transform criminals into delinquents, life-long criminals. Is not the structured and knowable 'failure' of the prison, a 'consequence rather than a contradiction' (272) of prison? Could it be that the purpose of imprisonment, the reason why the modern period turned so decisively to make all punishments result in imprisonment, is not to suppress criminal offences, but to allow them to be distinguished, distributed and made more broadly useful (272)?

Why would the prison system want to increase the production of criminals? Foucault's explanation for this is that this production was strategically useful for helping to establish and consolidate bourgeois domination. The impetus for penal reform in the late eighteenth century had been 'the struggle against illegalities' (273), but in spite of the codes that Foucault describes in Part Two on Punishment, a new 'popular illegality' began to develop in the movements between 1780 and the Revolution of 1848. This rising form of illegality was far more threatening than the older version of tolerated illegality, because the newer version was increasingly politicized and directed against middle-class rule. The modern forms of illegality from the Revolution onward increasingly 'linked together social conflicts, the struggles against the political régimes, the resistance to the movement of industrialization, the effects of the economic crises' (273). There was a three-fold process of politicized resistance in a new mode of illegality.

Firstly, Foucault speaks of 'the development of the political dimension of popular illegalities' (273). This change of perspective happened as previously local practices of resistance, like refusing to pay taxes, popular attacks on food hoarders and forcing shop-keepers to sell products for reasonable prices in times of shortages became, during this period, a feature of 'directly political struggles, whose aim was not simply to extract concessions from the state or to rescind some intolerable measure, but to change the government and the very structure of power' (273). In other words, popular resistance moved beyond seeking reforms to demanding revolution, and illegal practices were one manifestation of these demands.

Secondly, this 'political dimension of illegality' grew more complex as it became increasingly linked with and articulated into working-class struggles ('strikes, prohibited coalitions, illegal associations', 273) and the popular republican political parties that grew with every attempt by the state to restrict them through new laws. With this passage, the working class's fights were increasingly less against particular 'agents of injustice' (274) – the police, judges, or ministers – and more against the very concept of the law and justice itself, specifically the model of law and justice as established by the increasingly dominant bourgeoisie and their mode of capitalist production. After practising 'illegality' by resisting *Ancien Régime* laws, plebeians moved to a political recognition that the new bourgeois concept of liberal 'justice' was usually class-defined (for example with the laws against unions) and therefore justice was not neutral, but biased in favour of certain classes. Consequently, '[a] whole series of illegalities was inscribed in struggles in which those struggling knew that they were confronting both the law and the class that had imposed it' (274). The lower classes began to see criminals as their comrades, rather than alien others, in class struggles against the wealthy.

Lastly, the result of new forms of law put into place by state, landowners, or employers was to increase the 'occasions of offences' (275) and place individuals who would otherwise not have committed crimes into positions where they were either accused of doing so or had, willingly or not, turned to illegal activities. As authorities implicitly forced the 'honest' poor towards crime for survival, they unwittingly facilitated communication between different social groups, as those who normally would not have thought of themselves as similar to criminals began to align themselves more sympathetically with their fate.

With this 'threefold diffusion of popular illegalities' at the turn of the nineteenth century came their 'insertion in a general political outlook' and a new relationship between crime and 'social struggles' developed, even if Foucault does not see evidence of a full-fledged 'massive movement of illegality that was both political and social' (275). While 'the possible overthrow of power' was not inherent in all these forms of popular illegalities, 'a good many were able to turn themselves to account in overall political struggles and sometimes even to lead directly to them' (274).

Not surprisingly then, in this climate, the middle classes, throughout the first half of the nineteenth century, felt increasing anxiety about the working class as an 'immoral and outlaw class' (275). Foucault suggests that such fears facilitated a significant shift from the eighteenth century, which had felt that the interests or drives towards crime could belong to anyone, to a more explicitly class-coded concern that criminals overwhelmingly come from the lower classes.

Quoting from several legal sources written in the early nineteenth century, Foucault notes that 'law and justice' barely hide their 'class dissymmetry' (276). He argues that the middle class isolated 'one form of illegality' and helped 'to organize [it] as a relatively enclosed, but penetrable, milieu' (276). The form of illegality that it cultivates to neutralize the other, more political and popular forms of illegality, is 'delinquency' (277). Delinquency is 'an illegality that the "carceral system"' has cultivated and inserted into society as a tactic. 'In short, although the juridical opposition is between legality and illegal practice, the strategic opposition is between illegalities and delinquency' (277).

Thus, prison cannot be considered as failing when it produces the 'pathologized subject' of crime in the form of the delinquent, which is a 'specific type, a politically or economically less dangerous – and, on occasion, usable – form of illegality' (277). While those in favour of prisons might say that they want to diminish illegality, they actually, as Foucault claims, use the material architecture of the prison and its mechanisms of gaining knowledge over its inhabitants as a device to increase delinquency outside of prison. Why?

If the tight space of the prison is a laboratory for the creation of delinquency, middle-class interests can produce '[d]elinquency, controlled illegality,' to work on behalf of the 'illegality of the dominant groups' (279). What makes the transformation of illegality into delinquency 'useful' for middle-class and capitalist interests? Firstly, there are financial benefits, for instance through the prostitution industry or, more recently, arms or drug trafficking: 'the delinquent milieu was in complicity with a self-interested Puritanism: an illicit fiscal agent operating over illegal practices... the existence of a legal prohibition creates around it a field of illegal practices, which one manages to supervise, while extracting from it an illicit profit' (279–80).

Secondly, delinquents are useful because they act as a means for authorities to supervise the 'vague, swarming mass of a population' by inserting individuals within this population who can be forced to be informers, since they are in the post-penal phase of supervision of 'constant surveillance' (278) and vulnerable to being threatened with the loss of freedom and return to prison. Similarly, delinquents can insert illegalities, like prostitution or drug use, into working-class neighbourhoods in ways that can effectively disrupt their internal cohesion, by destroying families, for instance, and political organization by working-class activists. A more recent example might be how black civil rights was thrown off-track by the rise in heroin and crack cocaine dealing, which seems never to have been 'handled' properly by the police. Delinquents can also be sent as a labouring force to the colonies, although Foucault does not consider this the main factor.

Delinquency is also a useful way of destroying working-class and left-wing political resistance because delinquents have a 'political use' as police informers and *agents provocateurs* (people who stir up trouble for the police to react with force), as a clandestine, informal police force that can collect information on people and neighbourhoods otherwise impenetrable by the police (280). Delinquents also allow for 'the infiltration of political parties and workers' associations, the recruitment of thugs against strikers and rioters' (280), and here Foucault cites Marx's *Eighteenth Brumaire of Louis Napoleon* that describes how Napoleon's nephew seized power, in ways prescient of how twentieth-century fascist parties would arm and deploy thugs against left-wing and workers' parties. In sum, then, Foucault defines delinquency as 'a diversion of illegality for the illicit circuits of profit and power of the dominant class' (280).

Not only is the delinquent a useful tool for authorities to penetrate neighbourhoods that might otherwise be difficult for them, even physically, to enter, it is also a cheaper system of control as informal agents are not as costly as salaried ones. The other goal in producing delinquency is that it also justifies authority's power to control the whole population. Think about how 'folk devils' are created to remove civil rights. The idea of 'protecting' us from internet paedophiles or terrorists, for instance, opens the way for legislation that the police can read everyone's mail. Foucault says that the delinquency system allows for the 'documentary system' of gathering knowledge to be generalized from its operation in prisons to now be used on the entire population, thus presuming criminality as something that covers everyone. Delinquency acts as 'a political observatory'; it 'constitutes a means of perpetual surveillance of the population: an apparatus that makes it possible to supervise, through the delinquents themselves, the whole social field' (281).

To sum up, prison provides the justification for continuing to survey people after they are released, it acts as a recruiting ground for informers, brings offenders into contact with each other so that they have a network that will help place them outside, and it makes it difficult for criminals to be reintegrated into society, so that it becomes 'all too easy for former prisoners to carry out the tasks assigned to them' (282). Delinquency is produced by a combination of the prison and the police, and these three elements (police-prison-delinquency) form a 'structural feature' (282) of modern society.

To illustrate how this ensemble circulates through its various positions, Foucault cites two notorious nineteenth-century figures, Eugène François Vidocq (1775–1857) and Pierre François Lacenaire (1800–1836). Vidocq was an imprisoned criminal, who then became a police informant and spy, and finally the head of a state-sanctioned unit of plainclothes security police, many of whom he recruited as well from prison. Because Vidocq was also a pioneer in scientific criminology, he neatly represents the fusion of new social sciences and the political use of delinquency. Vidocq's position as former prisoner turned police chief illustrates delinquency's 'ambiguous status as an object and instrument for a police apparatus that worked both against it and with it' (283). For Foucault, Vidocq's career stands out as a point when 'delinquency, detached from other illegalities, was invested by power and turned inside out... the disturbing moment when criminality became one of the mechanisms of power' (283).

The second figure is Lacenaire, an executed petty criminal and murderer, who was also a poet. A bungling criminal, Lacenaire in prison was celebrated by French high society even as his fellow inmates considered him little better than an informant. Foucault sees him not only as the moment when illegality is transformed into delinquency, but also as the point where the middle classes sought to appropriate the cultural status of delinquency for themselves, by aestheticizing crime as something that can only be done well by the bourgeoisie. The purpose, here, is to contest the symbolic codes of criminality that the labouring classes were using and turn these ideas against the working class. Foucault says that '[i]t should not be forgotten that Lacenaire's celebrated death succeeded in muffling the echoes of Fieschi's attempt on the life of Louis-Phillippe; Fieschi, one of the most recent of the regicides, represented the converse figure of a petty criminality leading to political violence' (284). Giuseppe Marco Fieschi (1790–1836) was a Corsican petty criminal who came with forged papers to Paris and then became a follower of the Republican Society of Human Rights (*Société des Droits de l'Homme*), a group that suffered political repression after popular unrest. After Fieschi's failed attempt to assassinate the King, repressive laws were passed that made it easier to prosecute political dissidence and limited press freedoms. Foucault notes that it is not coincidental that the Fieschi affair took place just months before the government banned the use of the increasingly threatening chain-gang, which began to celebrate criminal resistance.

Lacenaire is celebrated, Foucault suggests, not only because he was a typical delinquent, but also because his middle-class background made him seem reassuring to the Parisian bourgeoisie, quite unlike the threat of a Fieschi. Vidocq's rise and Lacenaire's fall belong together as two elements of a process involving the creation of an 'illegality of the privileged' wherein the middle class begins to mythologize and aestheticize crime for itself, as with Thomas De Quincey's *Murder Considered as One of the Fine Arts*, which appeared in French in 1849 (originally in English in 1827).

Foucault now turns to describe means of resistance and struggles against the police-prison-delinquency system. Firstly, Foucault reminds us that it was not easy to separate delinquents from the rest of the population and 'maintain the hostility of the poorer classes to delinquents' (285). Authorities had to engage in extensive campaigns about moral behaviour to establish a split between the criminal underworlds and working-class communities. One way to generate hostility of the 'poorer classes' to delinquents was the barely disguised 'use of ex-convicts as informers, police spies, strike-breakers or thugs' (285). There was also an increasing severity of punishment against workers' efforts to seek better labouring conditions. The political leaders of labour movements were often given harsher sentences than 'regular' criminals and when the two groups were mingled in prison, the latter were given better treatment, so as to heighten working-class resentment against criminals.

Additionally, there was a 'patient attempt' by authorities to make delinquents seem always present and threatening, a feature that seemed to justify constant police surveillance (286). The journalistic crime reporting, often very sensationalized, helped stoke fears of this 'faceless enemy' (286). The mass-market crime novel presented criminals as belonging to 'an entirely different world', either a lower-class or insane subculture or high society. In all cases, the effect was to make criminals seem 'very close and quite alien, a perpetual threat to everyday life, but extremely distant in its origin and motives' (286). We might today want to compare how government tactics against 'terrorism' are similar in this regard.

This dual strategy worked as working-class newspapers began to attack penal labour, complained about middle-class philanthropy for criminals and grumbled about literature that celebrated criminals. But Foucault also insists that it never worked so successfully as to create a 'total break between the delinquents and the lower classes' (287).

For instance, while workers were hostile to delinquents, in the years between 1830 and 1850 that marked an increasing tempo of revolutionary energies, the working class battled against the concept and practice of 'penality'. Workers' newspapers often provided 'a political analysis of criminality that contradicted term by term' the languages of philanthropy and bourgeois journalism (287). The left-wing press instead reversed the equation and blamed the 'origin of delinquency' not on individuals but on a bourgeois dominated society.

Similarly, because criminal trials were public, they replaced the chain-gang's processional as an opportunity for resistance. Trial reporting became 'the occasion for a political debate' by left-wing journalists to 'denounce the general functioning of penal justice' (288) as a form of class warfare on the working class. These daily reports became a form of counter-'crime accounts' as the newspapers proclaimed the bourgeoisie and social inequality as the source of crime, something that the followers of utopian socialist Charles Fourier (1772–1837) were especially active in doing as, in a proto-anarchist fashion, they defended the use of crime as a preliminary form of popular uprising.

Foucault uses the example of how criminal trials became an opportunity for political debate to show that all systems of justice, including the disciplinary system, can be overcome. For instance, the King's terror and the eighteenth-century's sign system failed because labouring-class spectators turned against them. Similarly, discipline works only if we agree to be influenced by its normalizing terms.

Here Foucault introduces a fourth character in contrast to Vidocq, Lacenaire and Fieschi, the adolescent petty criminal and vagabond, Béasse, who insouciantly spoke at his trial and resisted the judge's attempts to make him into a delinquent by refusing to accept the efforts to shame him as someone outside of life's regularities and imposed docility. The Fourierist papers took up this case as a polemic against bourgeois assumptions.

While Foucault acknowledges that these explicitly politicized accounts were not completely representative of the workers' press, he does think that it finds an echo when late nineteenth-century anarchists 'posed the political problem of delinquency' and tried not simply to heroicize criminals, but to make a structural critique that looked to disentangle delinquency from its bourgeois network and reconnect it with a 'political unity of popular illegalities' (292) against the ruling classes. One means of resisting the latter would be to invert the terms and argue that it is the middle class who are the true criminals and degenerates of society because they live off the profits created from labour stolen from workers within exploitative conditions.

With this example, Foucault implicitly suggests that a radical critique of the class origins of the justice system, if combined with working-class resistance, can topple the system. Here might be his notion of how the university's (historical) researchers could provide rhetorical tools for labouring-class empowerment.

3. The carceral

Foucault ends *Discipline and Punish* with a section called 'the carceral'. He chooses this term because it is a broader one than 'prison', and he wants to use a more encompassing term, since he will end the study by arguing for the ways in which the disciplinary techniques that he has studied in the penitentiary have become more widespread throughout society. We live in what Foucault calls a 'carceral archipelago' (297), a wide horizon wherein we are normalized by a set of interlinked, but also semi-independent, institutions. This section acts as Foucault's suggestion that the prison was necessary to study as a classic model of disciplinary normalization, but that to focus our attack solely on prisons would be to miss how more widespread the problem is, and, furthermore, he adds that prisons are not even as important a device of social control today as they were in the nineteenth century.

He begins this summary by saying that if he had to pick a date when the carceral system becomes complete, he would choose neither the influential French penal code of 1810, which was then widely copied throughout Europe, nor the later regulations of 1838 or 1844 when influential books on prison reform came out. Instead, he chooses 1840, the opening of Mettray, a juvenile offenders institution. He opts for Mettray because it contains 'the disciplinary form at its most extreme' (293), with hierarchical self-regulation, constant supervision, work, reform-minded education and isolation for punishment.

The authorities at Mettray are 'technicians of behaviour: engineers of conduct, orthopaedists of individuality' (294) rather than simply judges, teachers, foremen, or substitute parents. Their job was 'to produce bodies that were both docile and capable' through observation and documentation (294). Mettray is an ideal example for Foucault since it links with, but is not explicitly part of, medical, educational and religious institutions. Hence Mettray represents the diffusion effect of procedures that have now spread outward to create a wider disciplinary network. Foucault considers the inauguration of Mettray as a threshold moment because it did not seek to justify itself as a humanitarian venture or one located in rational science, but one simply based on quantitative norms that appear innocent because they are neither subjective in the way that individual charity might seem, nor as cold as mathematic proofs, but something in between. Mettray is therefore aligned with the rise of the social sciences. The purpose of Mettray, Foucault reminds us, is the enactment of a 'disciplinary technique exercised upon the body' in order to create a knowable 'soul' and bring about the individual's 'subjection' (in the dual sense of being made submissive and a subject for a case study) (295). Foucault highlights that Mettray was a total institution in that it also trained the instructors, who, as students, were also caught in the webs of disciplinary pedagogy.

With all of the above, Mettray comes, perhaps not coincidentally, nearly in the same year that scientific psychology marks as its birth with Ernst Heinrich Weber's 1846 'Der Tastsinn und das Gemeingefühl' ['The Sense of Touch and Common Sensibility']. Weber's work sought to find quantitative measurements for physical sensations like pain, which initially seem difficult to classify. Foucault indicates that this turn to make classifications about feelings belongs to the early emergence of psychology, as part of a professionalization of 'discipline, normality and subjection' (296). Consequently, we see a new historical phase beginning, where 'power-knowledge' (296) is encased in medicine and psychiatry and supported by 'a judicial apparatus which, directly or indirectly, gave it legal justification' (296). These methods, in turn, proliferate throughout hospitals, schools, public administration and private enterprise, and their agents have increased in their number, credentials and power. Consequently, Mettray marks 'a new era' in the 'normalization of the power of normalization' (296), a moment when these disciplinary techniques become widely accepted, dispersed and apparently inoffensive.

After a section break, Foucault asks a rhetorical question: Why should Mettray appear as both the consolidation of discipline as well as the start ('the point of emergence') of something new if the contemporary method of prisons is still the same as that used in the nineteenth century? What justifies this new periodization? Foucault's answer is that Mettray marks something new for the reason that it was not simply a prison for youth. Mettray did contain juvenile offenders, but it also held youth who had, nonetheless, been acquitted of crimes – those who had been removed from their parents or were orphans. By mixing up those explicitly found guilty by courts and those who were otherwise innocent, Mettray exemplifies how disciplinary techniques moved beyond being only applied to criminals.

Disciplinary normalization goes beyond 'the frontiers of criminal law' to form what Foucault calls the 'carceral archipelago' (297). The reference is to Aleksandr Solzhenitsyn's *The Gulag Archipelago*, a multi-volume work published in the West from 1973, just before *Discipline and Punish*'s publication. Solzhenitsyn (1918–2008) referred to a network of labour/prison camps spread throughout the Soviet Union, and Foucault's allusion suggests that normalizing institutions likewise extend throughout Western society. The allusion works, also, as a reprimand to Cold War conservatives who argued for the superiority of the West's personal liberties against Soviet state regimes. Foucault, as we have seen, is somewhat doubtful that we are really free to be and do what we want in contemporary

Western society. The 'carceral' is the term Foucault uses to describe a society dominated by penitentiary techniques in realms beyond the actual prison that form 'a great carceral continuum' or 'carceral net' (297).

The rise of extra-penal incarceration, or even the application of penitentiary techniques into other regions, means that authorities no longer look for larger events like actual crimes, but are constantly watching for 'the slightest illegality, the smallest irregularity, deviation or anomaly, the threat of delinquency' (297). The extensions of disciplinary norms into social realms meant that the 'threat of delinquency' became operative even in otherwise non-legal matters. Some examples that Foucault gives for this seepage of discipline are the institutions for the poor, abandoned children, young women who sought protection against a future life of prostitution and abuse or juvenile reformatories. Discipline was also exercised by institutions that did not literally enclose people, but ones that often dispensed open-air life support: 'charitable societies, moral improvement associations, organizations that handed out assistance and also practised surveillance, workers' [housing] estates and lodging houses' (298). Many of these institutions treated the humans who used their services as if they were criminals and prisoners, simply because they lacked social power.

As carceral techniques spread from the prison through 'the entire social body' (298), Foucault indicates six main effects.

Firstly, it became increasingly easy to fall away from normal behaviour in one way or another, regardless of the actual severity of the act. With the growth of the network of institutions that 'by means of observation and assessment hierarchized, differentiated, judged, punished' (299), a 'continuous gradation' emerged where it became very easy to blur the distinctions between small misdemeanours or alternative lifestyles and more serious felonies. To be different, to not be 'normal', was treated the same as being guilty of severe crime. The blurring between 'the least irregularity and the greatest crime' (299) meant that 'the social enemy' were not those who explicitly threatened the central authority of the (regal) State, but those who were simply different and thus suspicious. To be an outsider, one not within socially accepted norms (including those who like alternative music and clothes, sexual pleasures, etc.) is now the same as being an enemy of the State, a position that deserves institutionalization. One can effectively be born delinquent even before any actual outlawed act occurs.

Secondly, the effect of the increased number of institutions that looked for slippages into this abnormality was that a web emerged where someone could easily pass from one institution to another. A 'disciplinary career' was made that shuttled subjects throughout their life through the chains of different institutions (300). Once marked out, a person could barely escape being moved from one site to the next, from the orphanage to the school, the poorhouse, the prison etc.: 'The delinquent is an institutional product' (301). In the eighteenth century, Foucault suggests, there was still a space of escape from the 'direct hold of power' (300) by authorities, because it was possible to hide in marginal underworlds or subcultures; in the disciplinary modernity, these gaps have vanished: 'the carceral network' does not allow for anyone to be 'outside' of its oversight because, as Foucault explained in the previous section, it has a use for abnormals as a lever to discipline everyone else and there are so many disciplinary centres that envelop society.

Thirdly, and 'perhaps the most important effect of the carceral system and of its extension well beyond legal imprisonment' is that it lowers the threshold of popular resistance to discipline, since its ubiquity makes discipline seem 'natural', 'legitimate' and unremarkable (301). Disciplinary normalization succeeds in making its power seem too small to complain about because it constantly uses the two registers of legal justice and extra-legal discipline in tandem. Since there exists an explicitly legal court system, we assume that modern justice and the legally sanctioned discipline outside of the courts are 'free of all excess and violence' (302) against our freedoms. The carceral (the overall extension of prison techniques beyond the prison) works to make legal punishments seem natural and unarbitrary, as they mirror what takes place outside the courts, while the courts often protect the power of non-juridical authorities.

Foucault argues that, because there is now so little difference between the 'latest institution of "rehabilitation"', where one goes to avoid prison, and prison itself, the 'power to punish is not essentially different from that of curing or educating' (303). By operating at every level of the social body and by mingling ceaselessly the art of rectifying and the right to punish, the universality of the carceral lowers the level from which it becomes 'natural and acceptable to be punished' (303).

He then reiterates his basic claims for why the carceral as a tactic was chosen. By making legal punishments seem natural, and providing a legal backing to discipline, the carceral makes the violence of authorities seem acceptable. It weakens the spirit of revolt in a time when 'the problem of the accumulation and administration of men first emerged' (303) within a full-blown capitalist society.

Foucault notes that the traditional question has been, 'how, before and after the Revolution, a new foundation was given to the right to punish' (303). The standard answer is the 'theory of the contract' (303), that is both the notion that citizens have signed an implicit agreement with the State on the latter's right to rule, but also the ideal of a market society where goods and services are exchanged through legally-bound contracts. Defenders of the liberal state and capitalist economy highlight the contract. But Foucault says that it is important to ask the opposite question: 'how were people made to accept the power to punish, or quite simply, when punished, tolerate being so' (303)? The theory of the contract cannot answer this with recourse to the fiction of a mythological irrevocable 'moment' when a 'juridical subject' signed over the power to others the right to control them. Foucault instead thinks that it was the pressure of the emerging 'carceral continuum' that 'constituted the technical and real, immediately material counterpart of the chimerical granting of the right to punish' (303). The carceral is the alibi and fusion of social coercion and constructed consensus.

The fourth effect of the carceral is the emergence of a new form of 'law' that mixes legal proscription with the desire to constitute normality. The effect of having the law work not only to repress crime, but also to participate in the production of good souls, is that there is a shift in the nature of judges, as they seek to punish less and 'rehabilitate' more according to norms. Whether or not we blame the intentions of judges, their turn to doctors, psychiatrists and criminologists was a result of the spread of the carceral.

Norming is now to be found everywhere; it is seen as the practice of teachers, doctors, social workers and so on, where 'each individual, wherever he may find himself' is subject to the rule of the normative over 'his body, his gestures, his behaviour, his aptitudes, his achievements' (304).

The fifth effect is that the 'multiplicity and close overlapping of the various mechanisms' of the carceral, which seeks to make humans useful and docile, has both received support from the social sciences and made them 'historically possible' (305). 'Knowable man (soul, individuality, consciousness, conduct, whatever it is called) is the object-effect of this analytical investment, of this domination-observation' (305).

Lastly, the universality of these mechanisms is the reason why it seems so difficult to reform the prison; our 'inertia' (305) comes from the fact that it is no longer *simply* the prison that needs reforming, but nearly all of civil society within a capitalist-dominated economy. But Foucault does not think that the carceral 'cannot be altered, nor that it is once and for all indispensable to our kind of society' (305). This good news, however, is somewhat tempered.

There are two processes that could give 'considerable restraint' on prisons (306). The first is anything that 'reduces the utility (or increases its inconveniences) of a delinquency accommodated as a specific illegality, locked up and supervised' (306). We might think that Foucault means popular resistance here, but oddly his examples come from 'the growth of great national or international illegalities directly linked to the political and economic apparatuses (financial illegalities, information services, arms and drugs trafficking, property speculation)' (306), activities that burst through the tight controls of disciplinary social space. The presence (and interplay) of profit to be had from narcotics, arms-dealing, real estate speculation and other kinds of financial crimes is too great to be threatened by the prior constraints of normalization. Similarly, when state taxation may provide mass public revenue, through the legal, albeit disreputable, sale of pornography, pleasure aids and contraceptives, the older nineteenth-century sexual class hierarchies, where prostitution was tacitly allowed, but only when it provided for a protected circle of bourgeois men, are less effective. Foucault suggests that just as the contemporary middle class destroys its nineteenth-century industrial mechanisms, when these processes themselves become obstacles to a developing, more enlarged phase of capitalism, so, too, do the older disciplinary techniques become abandoned in the late twentieth century. When the older moral irregularities can provide profit on a greater scale, thanks to the contemporary globalization of the marketplace, then certain fractions of the middle class break away and lose interest in policing moral boundaries. Again, Foucault makes an implied criticism about contemporary demands for the freedom of sexual promiscuity, drug use and end to censorship of glorified violence in films and television. Because these previously deviant acts can now make big profits, in ways formerly not possible in the nineteenth century's less globalized marketplace, the older moralizing controls of space, time and human traffic become less comprehensive.

The second aspect that makes prison-reform less crucial (but not necessarily less worthwhile) is simply that the prison has become a less significant node when so many other features of society 'assume an ever greater share of the powers of supervision and assessment' (306). If prison is a less powerful deterrent in our imaginations today, it is only because its functions now exist in so many other places. When norming is done by educators, social workers, etc., the 'specificity of the prison and its role as link are losing something of their purpose' (306). For Foucault, '[i]f there is an overall political issue around the prison' (306), it is not really about prisons, but rather the 'steep rise in the use of these mechanisms of normalization and the wide-ranging powers…they bring with them' (306).

Foucault does not end on so grim a note, though. He concludes his study with an anecdote of political resistance by quoting an 1836 passage from the radical Fourierist journal *La Phalange* that complains about the middle-class vision of society. In the bourgeois world, there are carceral institutions in the centre that are surrounded by penal and police authorities, and then these, in turn, are surrounded by financial corruption, industrial exploitation, a sensational press, a smug middle class and free-market competition, 'the ruthless war of all against all' (307).

Foucault chooses this example because it suggests not a (monarchical) central power, but a 'multiple network of diverse elements' and 'strategic distributions' (307). The 'notions of institutions of repression, rejection, exclusion, marginalization, are not adequate to describe… the formation of the insidious leniencies, unavowable petty cruelties, small acts of cunning, calculated methods, techniques, "sciences" that permit the fabrication of the disciplinary individual' (308). Although Foucault's model here is that of a highly dispersed form of power, he also gives an unambiguous indication that it is the bourgeoisie and their capitalist interests, 'commerce and industry' that have constructed the carceral network as a 'strategy' in the 'combat' between classes (308). With this reminder, Foucault concludes *Discipline and Punish* by suggesting that it will act as a contextual preface and 'historical background' to future studies on the 'power of normalization and the formation of knowledge in modern society' (308). Whether or not we agree that Foucault himself did enough to supply such work, we may, nonetheless, take up his invitation and challenge and continue the project for ourselves.

Suggestions for Further Reading

Best 'Next' Foucault to Read

Foucault, Michel. *The History of Sexuality: Volume I: An Introduction*. New York: Pantheon, 1978.
——. *Power/Knowledge: Selected Interviews and Other Writings, 1972–1977*. (ed.) Colin Gordon. New York: Pantheon, 1980.
——. *Power: Essential Works of Foucault, 1954–1984; Vol. 3*. (ed.) James Faubion. London: Penguin, 2002.

After Foucault's death, his annual lectures that were tape-recorded by students were edited for publication. At the time of this writing, the most pertinent three for readers of *Discipline and Punish* are these. The lectures often give clearer or more detailed explanations of *Discipline and Punish*'s passages.

Foucault, Michel. *'Society Must Be Defended': Lectures at the Collège de France, 1975–1976*. (eds) Mauro Bertani and Alessandro Fontana. New York: Picador, 2003.
——. *Security, Territory, Population: Lectures at the Collège de France, 1977–1978*. (ed.) Michel Senellart. Basingstoke: Palgrave Macmillan, 2007.
——. *The Birth of Biopolitics: Lectures at the Collège de France, 1978–1979*. (ed.) Michel Senellart. Basingstoke: Palgrave Macmillan, 2008.

Biographies of Foucault

Eribon, Didier. *Michel Foucault*. Cambridge: Harvard University Press, 1991.
Macey, David. *The Lives of Michel Foucault*. London: Hutchinson, 1993.

How to Read Foucault's *Discipline and Punish*

Miller, Jim. *The Passion of Michel Foucault*. New York: Simon & Schuster, 1993.

General Discussions of Foucault

Halperin, David M. *Saint Foucault: Towards a Gay Hagiography*. New York: Oxford University Press, 1995.

Hoy, David Couzens (ed.) *Foucault: A Critical Reader*. Oxford: Blackwell, 1986.

Veyne, Paul. *Foucault: His Thought, His Character*. Cambridge: Polity, 2010.

Accounts of Foucault's Prison Activism

Artières, Philippe, Laurent Quéro and Michelle Zancarini-Fournel (eds) *Le Groupe D'Information Sur Les Prisons: Archives D'une Lutte, 1970–1972*. Paris: Éditions de l'IMEC, 2003.

Bourg, Julian. *From Revolution to Ethics: May 1968 and Contemporary French Thought*. Montreal: McGill-Queen's University Press, 2007.

Brich, Cecile. 'The Groupe D'Information Sur Les Prisons: The Voice of Prisoners? Or Foucault's?' *Foucault Studies*. 5 (2008): 26–47.

Histories and Critical Studies of Crime, Deviance and Social Control

Bender, Thomas (ed.) *The Antislavery Debate: Capitalism and Abolitionism as a Problem in Historical Interpretation*. Berkeley: University of California Press, 1992. [classic debate over humanitarianism and class]

Davis, Mike. *City of Quartz: Excavating the Future in Los Angeles*. London: Verso, 1990.

Garland, David. *Punishment and Modern Society: A Study in Social Theory*. Chicago: University of Chicago Press, 1990.

Gatrell, V.A.C. *The Hanging Tree: Execution and the English People, 1770–1868*. Oxford: Oxford University Press, 1994.

Goffman, Erving. *Asylums: Essays on the Social Situation of Mental Patients and Other Inmates*. Garden City, NY: Anchor, 1961.

Greenberg, David F. (ed.) *Crime and Capitalism: Readings in Marxist Criminology*. Palo Alto: Mayfield, 1981.

Hall, Stuart, Chas Critcher, Tony Jefferson, John Clarke and Brian Robert. *Policing the Crisis: Mugging, the State, and Law and Order*. London: Macmillan, 1978.

Ignatieff, Michael. *A Just Measure of Pain: The Penitentiary in the Industrial Revolution, 1750–1850*. New York: Pantheon, 1978.

Johnston, Norman Bruce, with Kenneth Finkel and Jeffrey A. Cohen. *Eastern State Penitentiary: Crucible of Good Intentions*. Philadelphia: Philadelphia Museum of Art for the Eastern State Penitentiary Task Force of the Preservation Coalition of Greater Philadelphia, 1994.

Linebaugh, Peter. *The London Hanged: Crime and Civil Society in the Eighteenth Century*. London: Allen Lane, 1991.

Melossi, Dario. *Controlling Crime, Controlling Society: Thinking About Crime in Europe and America*. Cambridge: Polity, 2008.

——. (ed.) *The Sociology of Punishment: Socio-Structural Perspectives*. Aldershot: Ashgate, Dartmouth, 1998. [includes Durkheim's essay on crime and several essays on Rusche and Kirchheimer]

Melossi, Dario and Massimo Pavarini. *The Prison and the Factory: Origins of the Penitentiary System*. London: Macmillan, 1981.

Meranze, Michael. *Laboratories of Virtue: Punishment, Revolution, and Authority in Philadelphia, 1760–1835*. Chapel Hill: University of North Carolina Press, 1996.

Rothman, David J. *The Discovery of the Asylum: Social Order and Disorder in the New Republic*. Boston: Little, Brown, 1971.

——. *Conscience and Convenience: The Asylum and Its Alternatives in Progressive America*. Boston: Little, Brown, 1980. [rev. ed. New York: De Gruyter, 2002]

Rusche, Georg and Otto Kirchheimer. *Punishment and Social Structure*. New York: Columbia University Press, 1939.

Literary Studies' Use of Foucault

Alber, Jan and Frank Lauterbach (eds) *Stones of Law, Bricks of Shame: Narrating Imprisonment in the Victorian Age*. Toronto: University of Toronto Press, 2009.

How to Read Foucault's *Discipline and Punish*

Miller, D.A. *The Novel and the Police*. Berkeley: University of California Press, 1988.

Sedgwick, Eve Kosofsky. *Epistemology of the Closet*. Berkeley: University of California Press, 1990.

Tambling, Jeremy. *Dickens, Violence and the Modern State: Dreams of the Scaffold*. London: Macmillan, 1995.

Marxism and Foucault

Poster, Mark. *Foucault, Marxism and History: Mode of Production Versus Mode of Information*. Cambridge: Polity, 1984.

Shapiro, Stephen. *How to Read Marx's Capital*. London: Pluto Press, 2008.

Feminism and Foucault

Bell, Vikki. *Interrogating Incest: Feminism, Foucault and the Law*. London: Routledge, 1993.

Bordo, Susan. *Unbearable Weight: Feminism, Western Culture, and the Body*. Berkeley: University of California Press, 1993.

Diamond, Irene and Lee Quinby (eds) *Feminism and Foucault: Reflections on Resistance*. Boston: Northeastern University Press, 1988.

McLaren, Margaret A. *Feminism, Foucault and Embodied Subjectivity*. Albany: State University of New York Press, 2002.

McNay, Lois. *Foucault and Feminism: Power, Gender and the Self*. Cambridge: Polity, 1992.

Ramazanoğlu, Caroline (ed.) *Up Against Foucault: Explorations of Some of the Tensions Between Foucault and Feminism*. London: Routledge, 1993.

Sawicki, Jana. *Disciplining Foucault: Feminism, Power, and the Body*. London: Routledge, 1991.

Taylor, Dianna and Karen Vintges (eds) *Feminism and the Final Foucault*. Urbana: University of Illinois Press, 2004.

Web Sites

Foucault Studies. <www.foucault-studies.com>. [an academic on-line journal]

Michel Foucault Archives. <http://www.michel-foucault-archives.org>.
  [Centre Michel Foucault]
Michel Foucault Resources. <http://theory.org.uk/foucault/>.
Michel Foucault, Info. <http://foucault.info/>.
Michel-Foucault.com. <http://www.michel-foucault.com/>.
Welcome to the World of Michel Foucault. <http://www.csun.
  edu/~hfspc002/foucault.home.html>.

Index

Compiled by Sue Carlton